CONTENTS

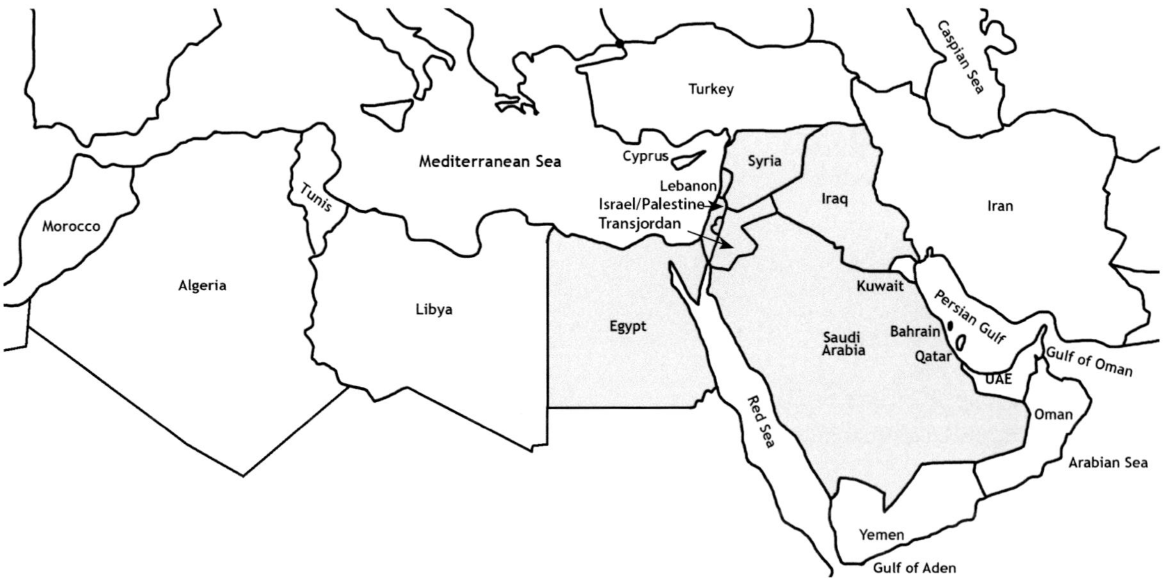

Helion & Company Limited
Unit 8 Amherst Business Centre, Budbrooke Road, Warwick CV34 5WE, England
Tel. 01926 499 619
Email: info@helion.co.uk Website: www.helion.co.uk Twitter: @helionbooks Visit our blog http://blog.helion.co.uk/

Published by Helion & Company 2024
Designed and typeset by Farr out Publications, Wokingham, Berkshire
Cover designed by Paul Hewitt, Battlefield Design (www.battlefield-design.co.uk)

Text © Dr. David Nicolle, Air Vice-Marshal Dr.Gabr Ali Gabr (EAF ret.) and Tom Cooper, with Waleed Miqaati and Nour Bardai 2024
Photographs © as individually credited
Colour profiles © Luca Canossa, Tom Cooper and Peter Penev 2024
Maps drawn by Paul Hewitt and Anderson Subtil © Helion & Company 2024

Every reasonable effort has been made to trace copyright holders and to obtain their permission for the use of copyright material. The author and publisher apologise for any errors or omissions in this work, and would be grateful if notified of any corrections that should be incorporated in future reprints or editions of this book.

ISBN 978-1-804514-24-5

British Library Cataloguing-in-Publication Data.
A catalogue record for this book is available from the British Library.

All rights reserved. No part of this publication may be reproduced, stored in a retrieval system, or transmitted, in any form, or by any means, electronic, mechanical, photocopying, recording or otherwise, without the express written consent of Helion & Company Limited.

For details of other military history titles published by Helion & Company Limited contact the above address, or visit our website: http://www.helion.co.uk. We always welcome receiving book proposals from prospective authors.

DEDICATION

For Air Commodore Abd al-Moneim Miqaati (8 July 1904 – 5 April 1982)
in memory of a meeting in Groppi's in 1970.

And there was gathered unto Soloman his hosts of Jinn and mankind and birds and they were set in bands. And when they came to the valley of the ants, an ant said: *Ants! Enter your habitations lest Solomon and his hosts may crush you while they perceive you not.*

(*Koran*, Sura 27 'The Ant', verses 17–18; tr. Abdul Majid Daryabadi [Markfield 2002]).
The Valley of the Ants, Wadi al-Naml, was traditionally located between Bayt Jibrin and the Palestinian coast.

ABBREVIATIONS

ALA	Arab Liberation Army (also referred to as the Arab Salvation Army)
ALC	Arab League Council
AMA	*al-Jihad al-Muqaddas*
BBC	British Broadcasting Corporation
GMA	*Al-Jaysh al-Jihad al-Muqaddas*
GMT	Greenwich Mean Time
RAF	Royal Air Force (British)
REAF	Royal Egyptian Air Force
RIrAF	Royal Iraqi Air Force
RJAF	Royal Jordanian Air Force
SyAAF	Syrian Arab Air Force
UN	United Nations
UNTC	United Nations Truce Committee

INTRODUCTION

THE ARABS GO TO WAR

This book, the tenth volume in the series *Air Power and the Arab World*, differs from previous volumes which were structured geographically or by air forces. This volume will present the initial phase of the Palestine War (First Arab-Israeli War or Israeli War of Independence) chronologically, this altered approach reflecting what was happening on the ground and in the air. However, while those Arab countries directly involved attempted some degree of political and military coordination, this largely failed – as would subsequent attempts to form a united front against what became the State of Israel.

It should be noted that references to 'the author' in connection with interviews, correspondence and other forms of personal communication refer to Dr. David Nicolle. Also note that the times given for Middle Eastern radio broadcasts as transcribed by the BBC Monitoring Service are GMT.

Several different conventions exist for the numbering of Spitfire variants. For the purposes of this work the fifth mark is referred to with the Roman numeral V, while the nineth and eighteenth variants are referred to with the Arabic numerals 9 and 18 respectively.

1

THE PALESTINE WAR BEFORE THE DECLARATION OF THE ISRAELI STATE (JANUARY–APRIL 1948)

The 'civil war' phase of the conflict in Palestine which erupted in November 1947, grew increasingly bitter and, on the Zionist side, more coordinated. On the Palestinian Arab side those who looked for help from the Arab states swung between optimism and frustration, the regional Arab leaders being reluctant to confront the UK which asserted that it would remain solely responsible for the administration of Palestine until the very end of the League of Nations, and now United Nations, Mandate on 15 May 1948. Furthermore, the Arabs still hoped that what they regarded as the obvious justice of the Palestinian cause would be recognised by the international community.

With intervention by several Arab states a conflict which began as a civil war would become a regular war which lasted for roughly 10 months. In fact, the Palestine War consisted of several phases, the first phase being the civil war from 1 December 1947 to 31 March 1948. This involved Palestinian irregulars and Arab volunteers on one side and several Zionist military organisations such as the *Haganah*, *Irgun tzeva'i l'eumi* and *Lohamei Herut Yisrael* on the other side. After the initial shocks of December 1947 wore off, the Palestinian irregulars and Arab volunteers held the initiative for about four months, mostly using guerrilla tactics, besieging isolated Zionist settlements and blocking the movement of Zionist supplies. Meanwhile Zionist military organisations had relatively little success and suffered significant casualties.

The second phase of the civil war lasted from 1 April to 14 May 1948 when the *Haganah*, having received several arms shipments, went on the offensive, seeking to consolidate the territory of the forthcoming Jewish state and to win control of more while British forces started to withdraw from Palestine. The fighting became more intensive and focused with Zionist military operations to seize strategic areas and important towns. By the end of this phase, Zionist forces had taken control of much of the territory allotted to the Jewish state under the UN Partition Plan. However, claims that Zionist forces advanced further into areas allocated to the Palestinian Arab state are misleading or insignificant. Meanwhile, substantial areas of the proposed Jewish state were still controlled by their local Arab inhabitants.

On 6 February 1948, the Arab Higher Committee informed the UN Secretary-General that Palestinian Arabs would never recognise the validity of the partition recommendations or the authority of the UN to make such a ruling. Secondly, the Palestinian Arabs regarded any attempt by the Zionists to establish a Jewish state in Arab territory as an act of aggression. Thirdly the Higher Committee stated that it would be pointless for any UN Commission to go to Palestine because no Arab would cooperate with it. Justified or otherwise, the Palestinian leadership had put itself at odds with the UN.

In January 1948, the Zionists launched Operation Zarzir to assassinate Palestinian leaders, and on the 21st of the month Sir Alexander Cadogan, the British representative to the United Nations Palestine Commission, summarised the situation as follows;

> In the present circumstances, the Jewish story that the Arabs are the attackers and the Jews the attacked is not tenable. The Arabs are determined to show that they will not submit tamely to the United Nations Plan of Partition; while the Jews are trying to consolidate the advantages gained at the General Assembly by a succession of drastic operations designed to intimidate and cure the Arabs of any desire for further conflict.

On the ground, the fighting became increasingly brutal with assassinations, the destruction of Arab homes, businesses, cafes, restaurants and hotels forming a central feature of Zionist military strategy. These horrors ranged across almost the entire country, including the Holy City of Jerusalem. There were also credible accusations of rape being used to terrify and humiliate the Arab population.

The violence as well as success of Zionist military actions during this period shocked the British authorities who were theoretically still in charge of Palestine. One of the most dramatic was the mining of the Cairo to Haifa railway line near Benyamina on 31 March, derailing an express passenger train carrying mostly Arab passengers with the loss of between 24 and 40 lives, with 61 injured. The al-Qantara to Haifa train had earlier been attacked on 27 February 1948, with 27 British soldiers being killed and 36 injured. On that occasion the RAF sent a section of Spitfires from No. 208 Squadron to search for the attackers, but without success. Then on the night of 3 April 1948 three ships named the *Hagana* (ex-Royal Canadian Navy *Norsyd*), *Josiah Wedgewood* (ex-Royal Canadian Navy *Beauharnois*) and *Noga* (ex-USS *PC-1265*) arrived in Tel Aviv with 200 machine guns and 4,300 Czech rifles hidden beneath what remained of a cargo of potatoes.

In military terms the Palestinians were clearly growing weaker while their foes grew stronger. During the second week of April 1948 Zionist forces rapidly gained the upper hand, Operation Dalet aiming to win control of all the major lines of communication between Jewish population centres, including those which lay within the proposed Palestinian Arab state. This resulted in more Arabs fleeing and was followed by intensified operations of ethnic cleansing of Arab inhabitants by Zionist forces. What had started as a civil war between the country's intermingled Arab and Jewish communities, became a struggle characterised by brutality on both sides, fuelled by reports of atrocities ranging from the true to the fantastic, massacre triggering massacre in a sequence of tit-for-tat retaliations. It also became a propaganda war as each side sought to win sympathy and support by highlighting the horrors it had suffered, while ignoring or downplaying the suffering of the other side. In such a war of information the Zionist cause enjoyed a clear advantage outside the Middle East whereas the Palestinian Arab narrative dominated the 'information war' within the Arab and to a considerable extent the wider Muslim worlds.

In military terms, the *Haganah* largely paralysed the Arab village militias in southern Palestine during Operation Nachshon (2–20 April 1948). It was during Operation Nachshon that, on 12 April, the *Egyptian Gazette* newspaper repeated a British report that a Zionist (or 'Jewish') reconnaissance aeroplane had been shot down over Kfar Zion in the Hebron area the previous day. The Jerusalem Corridor was also systematically conquered and its Arab population expelled.

This successful offensive, undertaken only weeks before the end of the British Mandate, caused a sudden deterioration in the Palestinian Arabs' military situation and resulted in thousands of Palestinians fleeing their homes or farms. This in turn led surrounding Arab populations to demand that their governments take more effective action. With Zionist forces gaining an ascendancy in Palestine, the UN Security Council reconvened on 15 April to an immediate ceasefire, though no decision was reached. Two days later the Security Council adopted resolution S/727 which established a Truce Commission composed of representatives from France, Belgium and the United States tasked with helping bring about a ceasefire.

On 16 April the General Assembly reconvened and on the same day Zionist forces launched another offensive, Operation Yiftach, in the north of the country, aimed at the conquest of eastern Galilee to enable existing Zionist colonies to prepare for an anticipated Arab invasion. Its success resulted in the destruction and emptying of Arab villages around Lake Hula. Fighting also broke out in Tiberias where news of nearby massacres prompted panic and on 18 April virtually the entire Palestinian Arab population was evacuated under British military protection.

Following the fall of both Haifa and Tiberias, Zionist forces turned their attention to Jaffa, the largest Arab City in Palestine with about 90,000 inhabitants, and the surrounding areas. The name Operation Chametz meant 'cleansing' in Hebrew and gave a foretaste of the fate of its Arab residents. In the event this ambitious, large-scale offensive proved to be particularly hard fought and also drew in reluctant British forces who were called upon to intervene to prevent Arab Jaffa being encircled. As a result, British artillery and the RAF targeted the Zionist settlement of Bat Yam, south of Jaffa and even threatened to take action against Tel Aviv. Also as a result, *Haganah* and British troops would face each other on the edge of Jaffa until the end of the British Mandate two weeks later. Even so a mass flight of the Palestinian population took place under British protection and when British troops finally left this area, the city of Jaffa which fell into Zionist hands had already been abandoned by the majority of its Arab population.

The assault on Jaffa was far from being the only Zionist military operation during April 1948, one of which was named 'Bi'ur Chametz' or 'Passover Cleaning'. This aimed to 'break the enemy in Haifa' by simultaneous assaults from several directions between 24–30 April. It is also worth noting that an estimated half of the total 700,000 or so Palestinian Arab refugees registered by the UN Refugee Agency after the conflict ended in 1949, had been driven from or fled from their homes before 14 May 1948; in other words, before the intervention by regular Arab armies.

The fighting in March and April again resulted in accounts of horrific brutality as well as the seemingly random killings which came to characterise some Zionist military operations. The most notorious was the slaughter at Dayr Yassin which, unlike most other atrocities, rang around the world. Some subsequent Israeli studies put the number of victims killed at 254. Only 50–70 were wounded and the proportion of killed to injured is one of the factors which identify the Dayr Yassin Massacre as a controlled and calculated act of terrorism. Reports of these horrors naturally reached the surrounding Arab countries and beyond, often being greatly exaggerated in the process. While the populations of independent Arab countries clamoured for their governments to do more – to do anything – such reports encouraged increasing numbers of Arab and other Muslim volunteers to seek to join the Palestinian struggle. As a result, the Gaza area was soon garrisoned by Muslim Brotherhood volunteers, largely from Egypt and the Sudan, commanded by Tarik al-Afriqi, an ex-Sudanese officer who had reportedly been born in Nigeria and who now established his HQ at al-Majdal, north of Gaza.

There were fewer accounts of such brutality on the Palestinian Arab side, perhaps partly because the Palestinians were on the defensive and teetering on the brink of collapse. Nevertheless, the worst Arab atrocity of the war, the massacre by irregular fighters of dozens of surrendering *Haganah* troops including some 20 women at Kfar Etzion just north of Hebron on 13 May, was not provoked by any immediate Jewish atrocity or attack in that particular area. Elsewhere, some Palestinian villages now fell without resistance as the Arab position deteriorated further during a series of Zionist operations whose Hebrew names sometimes reflected the fact they were, in reality, a form of ethnic cleansing. The urgency with which the Zionist political and military leadership wanted to expand the territory it controlled before the end of the British Mandate, also led to more than one operation being launched at the same time.

Despite being firmly against partition, the Palestinian leadership failed to set up quasi-governmental organisations. The existing Palestinian militias of the *Futuwa* and the *Najada* were merged into one paramilitary force called *al-Jihad al-Muqaddas* or AMA early in 1948. Nor were significant preparations made to defend territory the Palestinians currently held. Instead, committees were established to control war operations within specific vicinities. Thus, when serious military operations started, the Palestinian Arabs lacked the cohesion and effectiveness of the opposing *Haganah* and *Palmach* which rapidly became a proper army. The only effective Palestinian military force was the Arab Liberation Army (ALA) commanded by Fawzi al-Quwaqji. Consisting of local Palestinians as well as volunteers from across the Islamic world, its most efficient element included about 2,500 Syrians, 2,500 Iraqis, 500 Lebanese and 150 Bosnian Muslims.

The British government had, of course, already decided to pull its forces out of Palestine, and a gradual withdrawal of all RAF units had been planned. Aircrew and aeroplanes were to fly to Cyprus while the greater part of the RAF ground personnel would travel overland to Egypt, mostly to bases along the Suez Canal. Meanwhile a rear-guard would remain around Haifa, in what became the Haifa Enclave, until the British evacuation was otherwise complete. This enclave was actually quite extensive and included the RAF aerodrome at Ramat David, 30kms southeast of Haifa which would be the scene of almost the last act in the traumatic drama of the British occupation of Palestine.

On 5 May, the Hawker Tempests of No. 6 Squadron RAF also moved from Khartoum, via Wadi Halfa, to Fayid in the Suez Canal Zone, from where they would support the evacuation. Feelings in this British squadron were not particularly favourable to either side in the struggle between Palestinian Arabs and Jewish Zionist settlers, with various stories circulating which reflected current British prejudices. The following account in No. 6 Squadron's Operations Log Book followed a visit to the RAF airbase at Ramat David;

> Apparently a member pilot of 32 Squadron was approached by a wealthy looking Jew outside Ramat David and propositioned in a manner of low intrigue typical of the Jewish way in Palestine. The proposition was as follows; that the pilot should part with his aeroplane in favour of the Jewish Air Force for the Sum of £7,000 and that the amount to be paid into the banking account of the first party. The way in which the aircraft was to change hands was quite simple; the pilot would land at a Jewish held aerodrome, whereupon he would be put into the sea, "rescued" and taken to a hospital in Haifa, thus-wise he would be covered and exonerated.... At the time of going to press however, it is not thought that any pilots had suddenly become rich, and all our aircraft have returned safely!

In comparison to the carefully planned British withdrawal from Palestine, the military situation in the neighbouring Arab countries ranged from the moderately well prepared to the confused and almost chaotic. The question of armed intervention after the British withdrawal had of course, been discussed at many Arab League summit meetings but opinions remained deeply divided. While Syria and Transjordan were genuinely eager to intervene, Iraq and Lebanon were thought to sound more interventionist than they really were. Egypt and Saudi Arabia remained anti-interventionist until almost the last moment, the Egyptian government only being drawn in through fear of King Abdullah of Transjordan's clear desire to dominate Arab Palestine.

Back in 1947, when the Arab League Council (ALC) convened in Alayah in Lebanon from 7–10 October, the decision to defend Arab Palestine had resulted in the establishment of a Military Committee, headed by Iraqi former Chief of Staff, General Isma'il Safwat. Its report on Palestinian defence requirements highlighted the superiority of Zionist forces in manpower, arms and organisation whereas the Palestinian militias were ill-equipped, lacked military training and had no central command. General Safwat therefore urged the Arab states to mobilise their utmost strength and establish a general command while the Military Committee recommended the deployment of regular Arab forces close to the frontiers of Palestine.

A subsequent Arab League meeting in Cairo from 7–18 December 1947 was unable to decide upon effective measures to implement its decisions other than providing further financial and military support to the Palestinian militias. A force of 3,000 irregular volunteers known as the Arab Liberation or Salvation Army was, however, established and a few units from regular Arab armies were deployed near the Palestinian frontiers.

Initially most Arab leaders did not believe that the British government would really abandon Palestine but once they realised that this would actually happen they had three options:

1. to rely solely upon Palestinian irregular militias and Arab volunteers;
2. for Arab armies to intervene to establish an Arab State throughout Palestine;
3. to accept the UN Partition Plan and merge the Arab parts of a partitioned Palestine with the Kingdom of Transjordan.

Not until April 1948 was a clear decision taken concerning intervention by Arab regular forces, largely because the Palestinian militias and Arab volunteers enjoyed reasonable success until March that year, but also because most Arab leaders remained highly suspicious of King Abdullah of Transjordan's ambitions. In fact, King Abdullah was preparing to seize the Arab part of partitioned Palestine and had reached an agreement with the British Foreign Office on condition that Transjordanian forces did not invade areas allotted to the proposed Jewish state, an agreement unknown to other Arab governments.

Syrian troops with mule transport photographed in early 1948, perhaps on manoeuvres before being committed to the Palestine War. (Albert Grandolini collection)

At another ALC meeting in Cairo from 10–22 April 1948, King Abdullah offered to send his army to save Arab Palestine. This offer was accepted, but only on two unrealistic conditions; namely that the Transjordanian army, or Arab Legion, liberate the whole of Palestine and that the country would then be handed over to its own people and, by implication, their political representatives. Even then, the ALC still hoped that British withdrawal might be postponed and on 17 April Abd al-Rahman Azzam Pasha, the League's General Secretary, met the British Ambassador in Egypt in an attempt to delay the British withdrawal until an independent Palestinian Arab state could be established. Though Azzam Pasha indicated that the only alternative would be a full-scale war in Palestine, the British government remained determined.

On 29 April 1948, a further Arab League meeting in Amman included Arab military chiefs-of-staff. The latter declared that the minimum force required to overcome Zionist forces would be six infantry divisions and six fighter-bomber squadrons. This the political leaders refused to believe and instead instructed their militaries to prepare for intervention using only their existing and entirely inadequate forces. In fact, all Arab political leaders with the exception of the Transjordanians were out of touch with the real situation in Palestine.

On 11 May 1948, under pressure from the government of Iraq, from Azzam Pasha and from public opinion, the Egyptian government finally accepted the need for intervention in Palestine by Egyptian regular forces, not only to defeat the emerging Jewish state but to thwart King Abdullah's ambitions. Only when the ending of the British Mandate was imminent, was it at last decided that intervention would begin immediately, on 15 May 1948. Continuing suspicion and discord also meant that the Arab governments failed to establish a unified general command or even a general staff council. Only at the last moment was King Abdullah chosen as the nominal Commander in Chief with Major General Nur al-Din Mahmud, the Iraqi Chief of Staff, as his Deputy.

There were, of course, already non-Palestinian Arab and Muslim volunteers inside Palestine, notably those Muslim Brotherhood units led by Tarik al-Afriqi who was based at al-Majdal north of Gaza. In general, however, the Zionist forces already held the initiative. On 10 April a light reconnaissance aeroplane of the Sherut Avir, the air arm of the *Haganah*, identified an Arab artillery battery between Ma'aleh Ha'Chamisha and Jerusalem which was assumed to have been operated by the Egyptian Army.

In fact, Egyptian soldiers, including a handful of officers or NCOs, had entered the country amongst Muslim Brotherhood volunteers. On 28 April a quasi-official unit of Muslim Brotherhood volunteers under an Egyptian Army officer, *Qa'im Makam* Ahmad Abd al-Aziz Bey also left Cairo for al-Arish and crossed the frontier a fortnight before the Egyptian Army's official intervention. Referred to as 'commandos' in the Egyptian press, their duties would include liaising with local Palestinian militias and other volunteer groups. In the meantime, Abd al-Aziz Bey's men headed towards Hebron and Bethlehem to prepare for a possible link-up between Egyptian and Transjordanian Arab Legion Armies near Hebron after the British Mandate ended.

The somewhat loose military plan drawn up by the Arab states envisaged the armies of Iraq, Syria, Lebanon, and Transjordan meeting somewhere in the central part of the UN-designed Arab state of Palestine. Those of Egypt and Transjordan aiming for the point of confluence where the four main sections or divisions of central and southern Palestine (two Arab and two Zionist) as designated by the UN Partition Plan came together between Isdud and Qastina – thus very near the little town of Falujah.

The only regular Arab forces to enter mandated Palestine before the end of the British Mandate on 15 May 1948 were from Transjordan's Arab Legion, which 'jumped the gun' even according to the Arab League's ill-defined plan. This resulted in the Battle of the Etzion Bloc (12–13 May 1948), a relatively closely-packed group of four Zionist settlements. Glubb Pasha, the CO of the Transjordanian Arab Legion, feared that the garrisons of these and other Zionist settlements near Hebron might cut the road between Jerusalem and Egypt, blocking a convoy of much-needed ex-British military equipment from Egypt to Transjordan which was due to arrive on 13 May. The result was a hard-fought battle in which Zionist aircraft dropped supplies to the besieged garrison, their parachutes being mistaken for those of paratroopers by some Arab observers. After the final Etzion settlement surrendered and Arab Legion troops pulled back, villagers from the Hebron district stormed the area, murdering an estimated 240 settlers along with *Haganah* and *Palmach* fighters who had surrendered, including about 20 women.

The killings which followed the fall of the Etzion Bloc, and the failure of the Arab Legion to protect those who had surrendered, was undoubtedly a war crime. The destruction of the Etzion Bloc and the deaths of so many of its inhabitants and defenders also led to a change in Zionist-Israeli military policy which had previously insisted on defending outlying settlements 'to the last man'. With Arab regular armies poised to intervene, the *Haganah* command realised that several isolated positions would probably be unable to hold out against attack by regular troops.

2
FORCES AND STRATEGIES

On Friday 14 May 1948, an hour before the British Mandate was due to expire at midnight, the UN General Assembly convened to consider another draft resolution submitted by the committee dealing with the worsening situation in Palestine. By then, however, David Ben-Gurion had announced in Tel Aviv that the State of Israel had formally come into existence at 1600 Tel Aviv time (1000 New York time and eight hours before the official end of the British Mandate).

Without consulting the American State Department or informing the American delegates to the UN, President Harry S. Truman promptly recognised the new Jewish state. Also on 14 May 1948, the Egyptian government announced that Egyptian forces had been ordered to restore order and 'stop the slaughter that the Jewish forces are perpetuating against the Arabs.' From Cairo's point of view, the role of the other Arab armies seemed merely to support the Egyptians who were hardly expected to have to fight. Furthermore, Egypt wanted to be recognised as the leading power in the Arab League, while King Faruq believed that military success in Palestine would strengthen his own position within Egypt.

In fact, the First Arab-Israeli War, Palestine War or Israeli War of Independence, would not be a straightforward contest between opposing forces. Instead, it would be repeatedly interrupted by ceasefires imposed by the UN Security Council and accepted, with varying degrees of willingness, by the competing sides. It would also be a disaster for the Arabs as a whole, for the Palestinians in particular, and for almost all those Arab leaders involved.

At the start of this 'official' Palestine War, as distinct from the preceding civil war phase, the Arab governments still had no strategic plan other than 'keeping Palestine as an Arab country' and 'taking decisive measures to defeat the UN Partition Plan.' Militarily, all that existed was an agreement that the Egyptian forces were to occupy al-Majdal and Asqalan (Ashkelon), securing their right flank at Bir al-Saba (Beersheba) and establishing Arab control over the north-western part of the Negev Desert. The Lebanese contingent was to separate the northern Zionist settlements from Haifa and to link up with Syrian forces approaching from the east. The latter were to isolate Zionist-held Safad and Zionist settlements as far as Lake Tiberias, separating them from the rest of the country. A joint Iraqi and Transjordanian strike-force was to advance across the river Jordan to al-Afulah, cutting Zionist communications between Haifa and Baysan, and between Baysan and Tel Aviv.

Then, at the last moment, King Abdullah as nominally overall Arab commander took Glubb Pasha's advice and changed his troops' objectives. Consequently, the main Egyptian force was only supposed to advance along the coastal road as far as Gaza while the Egyptian navy, supported by the Royal Egyptian Air Force (REAF), watched the Palestinian coast. In the meantime, however, an Egyptian Light Force was to advance through Bir al-Saba (Beersheba) to secure al-Khalil (Hebron) and link up with King Abdullah's Arab Legion, preliminary elements of this Light Force having already crossed the frontier into the UN-designed Arab area of the Negev on 6 May.

There were also last-minute changes where other Arab forces were concerned. The Lebanese contingent was now to advance against the 'finger of Galilee,' a strip of north-eastern Palestine between Lebanese and Syrian territory, take control of the area and link up with local Arab Liberation Army forces. The Syrians were now to cross the Jordan south of Lake Tiberias, to seize Samakh and establish a bridgehead. The Iraqis were now to move from their assembly area in north-western Transjordan, take control of an area west of the Mijama'a Bridge and established another bridgehead west of the Jordan. This revised plan gave the leading role to King Abdullah's own troops who now had two objectives. One infantry brigade should take control of Nablus and a mechanised brigade was to advance to Ramlah while a third brigade remained in reserve. These last-minute changes also offended King Faruq of Egypt who felt almost sidelined.

Meanwhile, as fighting continued between Palestinian Arabs and Zionist settlers, the British evacuation of Palestine proceeded. The RAF's Nos. 6, 32 and 208 Squadrons ensured that two road columns could move safely from Jerusalem and al-Sarafand into Egypt. On their day of departure (incongruously called D-Day), No. 6 Squadron would fly 18 sorties providing continuous air cover from first light. For the rest of May this squadron would fly reconnaissance and escort missions, its last sortie being to escort a Dakota carrying the UN Mediator, Count Folke Bernadotte.

The RAF left Jerusalem on 12 May, its HQ being handed over to the British Army until the latter also withdrew, while the Air Officer Commanding and his staff moved to nearby Qalandiya (Kulundia) airfield. Next day various other British forces were taken by ship from Haifa, including 500 men of the paramilitary Palestinian Police Force. D-Day was set for 14 May and would see the departure of all remaining British military and civilian personnel except those holding the Haifa Enclave. The last British High Commissioner for Palestine, General Sir Alan Cunningham, was driven from Jerusalem to Qalandiya and then flown to Haifa. The remaining members of the British civilian administration were flown from Qalandiya to Ramat David.

At this point the road convoys set off under the protection of RAF No. 6 Squadron's Tempests from Fayid in Egypt, and Nos. 32 and 208 Squadron's Spitfire 18s from Ramat David in northern Palestine. The convoy from Jerusalem followed the inland road through al-Khalil (Hebron) and Bir al-Saba (Beersheba) to the Egyptian frontier while the convoy from al-Sarafand took the coastal road through Gaza. After an overnight stop, both convoys set off again on 15 May, the same day that Egyptian forces started moving in the other direction into Palestine. In fact, a section of RAF No. 32 Squadron Spitfires reportedly saw a number of REAF Spitfires, either on their way to strike Israeli targets or carrying out reconnaissance.

Thereafter, the enclave enclosing Haifa port and Ramat David aerodrome, where RAF squadrons were still based, was all that remained under British control. It may have been an inglorious episode in British history, but it was carried out with precision. Nevertheless, the British withdrawal without transferring administrative authority to any widely recognised body put the Palestinian Arabs at a significant disadvantage and left the country in a state of virtual anarchy. From the Arab point of view, this amply justified a military intervention in support of the embattled Palestinian Arabs, which they did with a total of around 15,000 troops, the overwhelming majority being infantry (14,426 men in 12 battalions).

MILITARY STRENGTHS

Palestine

The two paramilitary Palestinian Arab forces currently confronting Zionist forces were *Al-Jaysh al-Jihad al-Muqaddas* (widely known in Western sources as the GMA because of the use of the Egyptian pronunciation of both *jaysh* and *jihad*) under the supervision of the Arab Higher Committee, and the Arab Liberation (Salvation) Army or ALA. The GMA consisted of about 10,000 volunteers, a minority of whom had been given some formal military training by the British during their service in police units. The GMA nevertheless lacked a centralised command while its organisation consisted of small groups based in villages or towns. The largest such groups were deployed in and around Jerusalem under Abd al-Qadir al-Husaini. All lacked heavy weapons or logistic infrastructure, the GMA's arms consisting of 23 mortars, about 700 light machine guns and about 5,400 mostly old rifles. Lacking any form of military industry, the GMA was limited to the manufacture of primitive home-made munitions.

A rotund and not particularly youthful Palestinian irregular sporting a decorated leather pistol holster in 1948. (Albert Grandolini collection)

The second military force was the Arab Liberation (Salvation) Army, formed and trained outside Palestine under the supervision of General Isma'il Safwat who established his HQ in Qudsaya, just north-west of Damascus. General Safwat also set up four military commands to supervise Arab military actions inside Palestine: the Northern Command led by Fawzi al-Quwaqji whose responsibilities extended from the Syrian and Lebanese frontiers to Nablus and was also theoretically in overall command within Palestine; the Jerusalem Command led by Abd al-Qadir al-Husaini who also led the GMA in and around Jerusalem, his responsibilities also covering Ramallah, Bayt Lahm (Bethlehem) and al-Khalil (Hebron); the Lydda-Ramlah command allocated to Hassan Salama whose responsibilities extended as far as the outskirts of Jaffa; the Gaza-Negev Command led by Muhamad Tarik al-Afriqi of the Muslim Brotherhood; the Haifa Command under Adil Najm, an Iraqi officer; the Jaffa Command under Muhammad Hamad al-Hinayty, a Transjordanian officer.

By May 1948 the ALA initially numbered around about 7,700 volunteers including many from further afield, organised into eight battalions. In practice, however, the size and structure of the ALA was constantly changing, its units being reorganised and redeployed several times even during the first phase of the Palestine War. Al-Quwaqji also lacked a military staff and a reliable communication system, resulting in a lack of control and coordination. Furthermore, it had only six 75mm guns, a few mortars and 250 rifles for each battalion.

Early on January 1948, after a brief period of military training in Syria, the first ALA detachment infiltrated into Palestine and al-Quwaqji established his command post in Tubas between Nablus and Jinin. During April 1948, he had six battalions around Tubas, Nablus, Jinin and Baysan while two other battalions were deployed around Safad, Acre and Nazareth under another Syrian officer, Adib al-Shishakly. But by the end of May, all ALA units were again redeployed in the northern area under Fawzi al-Quwaqji.

Egypt

Prior to King Faruq's decision to send its troops across the frontier into Palestine, the Egyptian Expeditionary Force deployed around al-Arish was the largest and most powerful of the Arab forces committed to the Palestine War. Nevertheless, the smaller Transjordanian Arab Legion is generally considered to have been more effective, as least in some respects. Led by Major General Ahmad Ali al-Muwawi, the Egyptian Expeditionary Force numbered around 5,000 troops organised into one infantry brigade group, one 'light tank' battalion, one reconnaissance battalion, one artillery regiment (25-pdr field guns), an artillery battery with 18-pdr guns, a light anti-aircraft battery with 40mm guns, heavier anti-

Lynda Mas'ud, the famous female Egyptian pilot, with various Egyptian Army and REAF officers during the Palestine War, reportedly at a beachfront restaurant in Alexandria. (Tewfik family archive)

A lorry-mounted Bofors anti-aircraft gun of the Egyptian Army in Palestine. The practice of installing guns on trucks – to create the so-called 'portees' – was adopted from the British 8th Army of the Second World War fame. (Dr. David Nicolle collection)

aircraft units with 3.7-inch guns, a searchlight battery, engineering, technical and administrative elements. There was also one anti-tank battery with 6-pdr guns but, according to the Egyptian Army archive, the Egyptians did not know that the Israelis had any tanks, and the Egyptian Command ordered units heading east towards Falujah to leave their anti-tank weapons at Isdud. In the event, the battalion commander took two anti-tank guns on his own initiative, and these would save the day when Israeli tanks first appeared. The Egyptian Expeditionary Force was also joined by some Sudanese and Saudi Arabian companies.

A force of Muslim Brotherhood volunteers had already crossed into Palestine early in April 1948. A few weeks later, after the Egyptian Government permitted active participation in support of the Palestinian Arabs, a further 124 military men and 220 civilians volunteered to join this Muslim Brotherhood unit, along with 297 Libyans and 45 Tunisians. Now given official recognition as the Egyptian Light Force and commanded by *Qa'im Maqam* (Lieutenant Colonel) Ahmad Abd al-Aziz of the Egyptian Army's cavalry, it was secretly supported by some elements of Egyptian Army's artillery. These additional units crossed the frontier on 6 May 1948. As a result, the Egyptian Light Force was armed with four artillery pieces (3.7-inch), four anti-tank guns (2-pdr), eight machine guns and 106 rifles, reinforced over the next five weeks by 13 mortars, three heavy machine guns, eight light machine guns, 68 anti-tank rifles and 394 rifles. In the weeks and days before the main Egyptian Expeditionary Force crossed the frontier, the original Muslim Brotherhood volunteers and the Light Force gained valuable information and practical experience of confronting their enemy. This they and their officers then offered to the regular Egyptian Army, which apparently largely ignored it.

Transjordan

According to Egyptian military archives, the Transjordanian Arab Legion assembled 4,500 men in four battalions before crossing the river Jordan into Palestine. They were commanded by Brigadier General Norman Oliver Lash, a British police officer who had been seconded to the Arab Legion. The Legion's Chief of Staff remained Glubb Pasha who was supported by several other British officers including Ronald Joseph Callender Broadhurst, an Arabist scholar and later a Northern Irish politician. Nor would these foreigners lead from behind; the name of at least one British soldier being included in a list of fallen at the Martyr's Memorial in Amman. There were only five senior Arab officers in this force: Lieutenant Colonel Sidqi al-Jundi who commanded the 4th Brigade, Commander Habis al-Majally in charge of the 4th Battalion, Deputy Commander Abd al-Halim al-Sakit who commanded the 5th Battalion, Deputy Commander Abdullah al-Tal who commanded the 6th Battalion, and Deputy Commander Ali al-Hayary, a staff officer.

Two lorries carrying Syrian infantry or Palestinian irregulars in 1948. (Albert Grandolini collection)

Apart from garrison companies, the Arab Legion was well equipped, had received good tactical training and had an adequate stock of small-arms ammunition. In contrast, the Legion only had first-line ammunition for its mortars and artillery, lacking much if anything of a strategic reserve. Nor had Transjordan yet established an air force other than a handful of light aircraft belonging to the Arab Legion.

The Arab Legion force sent into Palestine thus consisted of two brigades comprising four motorised (lorry-mounted) infantry battalions, two artillery batteries each of four 25-pdr field guns, and seven garrison companies. Two battalions had already been deployed west of the Jordan on 13 May 1948 during the final phase of the British evacuation of Palestine but most were withdrawn on the 14th as part of the overall British withdrawal plan.

Iraq

Less information is available where Iraqi forces are concerned and that from available Egyptian Army archives lacks much detail. The force already in the area of al-Mafraq in Transjordan had numbered around 2,500 men led by Brigadier General Muhamad al-Zibaidy and consisted of two infantry battalions of three infantry regiments, one of which was mechanised, plus an armoured car battalion, an artillery battalion (25-pdr field guns) and an anti-aircraft artillery battalion.

Syria

Egyptian archives are more precise where the Syrian military commitment is concerned. It was led by Colonel Abd al-Wahab al-Hakim and consisted of 1,876 men in two battalions forming an infantry brigade, one mechanised infantry battalion and one artillery battalion (75mm guns). As of late April and early May, it was deployed near the Palestinian frontier, on or behind the Golan Plateau. The Syrians would also take the opportunity of the First UN Truce to assess their own performance. Here the infantry was found to be disappointing, so the Syrian government would set about recruiting amongst the Circassian population which was largely concentrated on the Golan Heights. Where military supplies were concerned, the Syrian situation was even worse than that of other Arab forces.

Lebanon

Of all the Arab forces committed to the struggle in Palestine, the Lebanese contribution was the smallest, with just one infantry brigade of around 1,000 men. Commanded by Brigadier General Fu'ad Shihab, it consisted of two infantry battalions supported by an artillery battery (75mm guns). Like Transjordan, Lebanon did not yet have an air force.

Israel

On the other side, the Zionists had different problems and advantages. The *Haganah* (precursor to the Israeli army until it was reorganised to become the core of the Israel Defence Forces on 28 May 1948) included three formations facing the southern frontier. These were the 12th Negev Brigade south of al-Khalil (Hebron) responsible for the area west as far as the road to al-Majdal, the 5th Givati Brigade in the area north of the 12th Negev Brigade, and the 7th Brigade in the foothills to the east. Not until August 1948, during the Second UN Truce, was an overall commander appointed for this southern region. Following recent successes against Palestinian militias and the volunteer forces supporting them, *Haganah* morale was high. However, its organisation was inflexible, each brigade being territorially based while its armoury remained light. Numerically the two sides were evenly matched, except in the very deep south, in the Negev desert where the Egyptians initially outnumbered *Haganah* troops by approximately two to one.

Troops of the Syrian Arab Army with an unidentified type of light tank or tankette in Palestine 1948, probably early during the Palestine War. (Albert Grandolini collection)

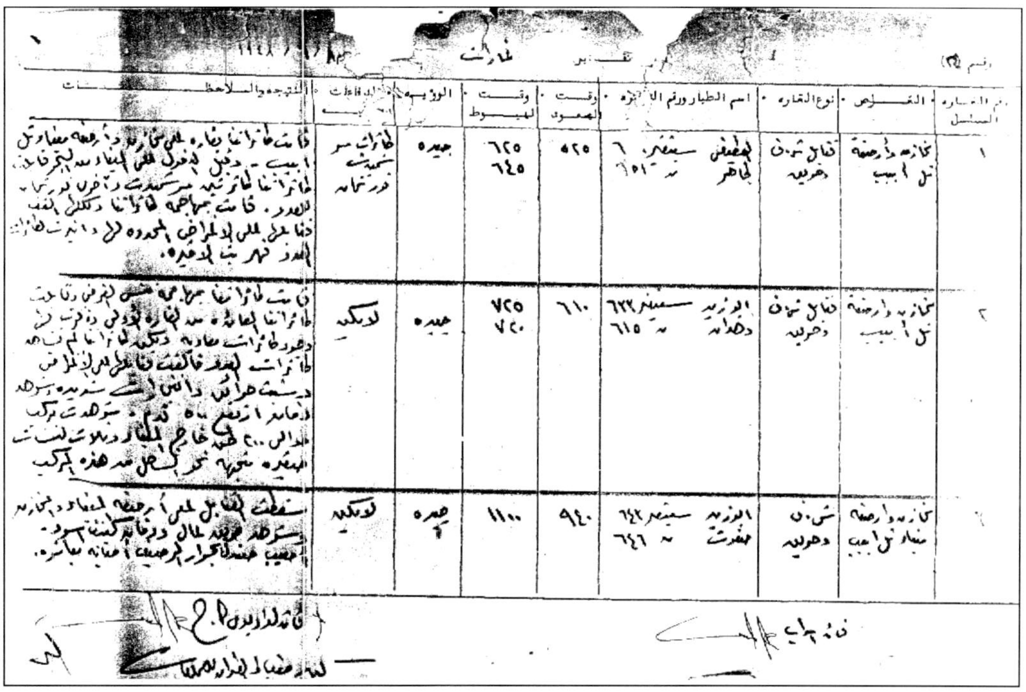

The first available page of the REAF Tactical Air Force's Operational Diary: page 48-6-8 (8 June 1948). (Dr. David Nicolle collection)

AIR FORCES

Royal Egyptian Air Force

Generally speaking, the Arab air forces flew in direct support of ground operations, though there would be a broader reconnaissance and even a strategic effort. There would also be some limited attempts by the REAF to airlift troops across enemy-held territory but the main role of the REAF's transport aircraft was to carry men and material over the British dominated Suez Canal area to the REAF's Tactical Air Force's only 'front-line' aerodrome at al-Arish.

Although the first pages of the REAF Tactical Air Force's Operational Diary are not available for research, there are more other sources available for the initial period of REAF operations over Palestine than there are for later periods. It is therefore possible to draw up a provisional list of 12 Egyptian Spitfire pilots who were apparently based at al-Arish during the first week of the 'official' Palestine War. They were: *Qa'id Asrab* Muhammad Abd al-Hamid Abu Zaid, *Qa'id Sirb* Mahmud Barakat, *Qa'id Sirb* Sa'ad Sadiq al-Duwayni, *Qa'id Sirb* Abd al-Rahman Inan, *Tayyar Awal* Gamal Irfan Sayf al-Nasr, *Tayyar Thani* Abd al-Karim Muharram, *Qa'id Asrab* Muhammad Nasr al-Din Zaghlul, *Qa'id Asrab* al-Qarmuti, *Qa'id Sirb* Tutmos Kamil Ibrahim Gibri'al, plus Tahir Zaki, Muhammad Safwat, probably Jalal Zaki, a pilot referred to as Mustafah Mustafah, and perhaps Ali Sharmi, who all held the rank of *Tayyar Thani*.

During the First Phase of the War, the Arabs achieved air superiority and forced the tiny Israeli Air Force to operate almost solely by night. Nevertheless, due to their lack of reserves and spares, the Arabs – with the possible exception of the Egyptians – could not afford to lose any aircraft, and certainly not any aircrew. For the Egyptians, the loss of four Spitfires and their pilots (three killed and one captured) on 22 May would come as a major blow, not least in morale terms. Before this disaster, the greater number of Egyptian aeroplanes and aircrew meant that the REAF could carry out significantly more combat sorties than its colleagues. It continued to do until the end of this First Arab-Israeli War. Nevertheless, initial Arab plans for their air campaign were unspecific and most sorties were launched in response to an immediate tactical need.

Table 1: REAF, Order of Battle, May 1948

Unit	Base	Equipment	Remarks
Royal Flight	Almaza	Anson, Lysander, Magister, Dakota	
No. 1 Squadron	Almaza	Spitfire LF.Mk 9	
No. 2 Squadron	Almaza	Spitfire LF.Mk 9	
No. 3 Squadron	Almaza	Anson, Lysander, Dakota, Magister	including Bomber Flight with 5 modified Dakotas
No. 4 Squadron	Dakhailah	Anson Mk I	
No. 5 Squadron	-	no aircraft	
No. 6 Squadron	Hilwan	Spitfire Mk Vb/c	
No. 7 Squadron	Almaza	C-47	plus C-46s in the process of overhaul
No. 8 Squadron	Almaza		bomber unit; working up
Flying School	Khanka	Magister	
Flying School	Hilwan	Harvard/Texan	
Flying School	Almaza	Harvard/Texan, Hurricane MkI/IIc, Spitfire Mk Vb/c	
Meteorological Flight	Almaza	Hurricane	

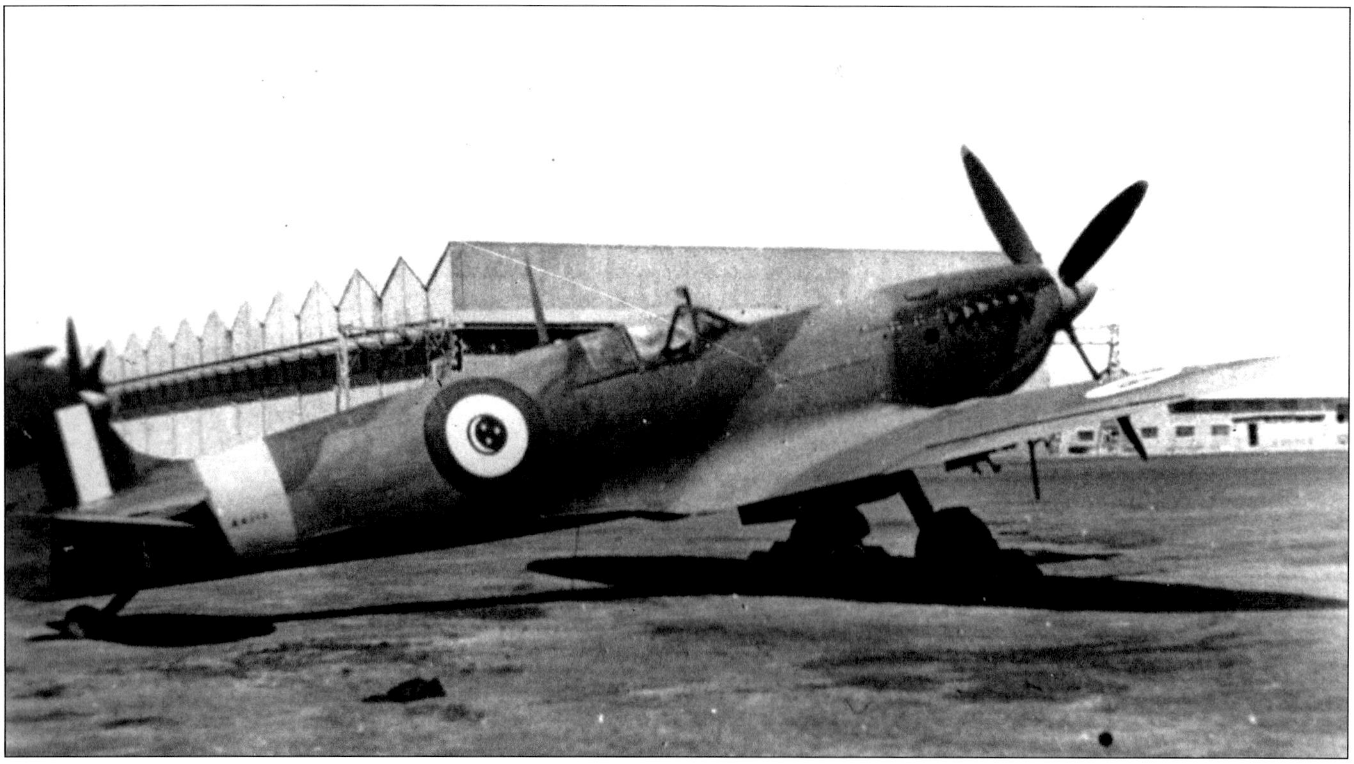

A Spitfire LF.Mk 9 seen shortly after delivery to REAF in early 1946. (Dr. David Nicolle collection)

A row of three Spitfire LF.Mk 9s seen on their handover to the REAF. Notable is the fresh coat of paint on all three examples and also their spinners and fuselage bands applied in white. (Dr. David Nicolle collection)

A REAF Spitfire Mk V landing, probably at Hilwan or Almaza, rather than al-Arish. (Dr. David Nicolle collection)

Royal Iraqi Air Force

In the early part of 1948, the RIrAF had a strength of 101 officers, of whom 95 were aircrew, plus 1,066 other ranks. Only part of this strength was committed to the Palestine conflict, those units which were involved being based at Mafraq in northern Transjordan. Here some of No. 7 Squadron's Avro Ansons would remain for several months under the command of Lieutenant

One of the REAF's old Miles Magister primary trainers (serial number L234, repeated in Arabic as '34T'), seen in the late 1940s. (Dr. David Nicolle collection)

Taylorcraft Austers of the Royal Iraqi Air Force, including serial number 224 (within a sequence generally thought to have been allocated to the Iraqi Air Force's Avro Ansons). (Albert Grandolini collection)

One of the first batch of De Havilland DH.104 Doves delivered to the REAF in 1947. They wore serial numbers Z900 to Z906, though the prefix Z was soon dropped, as clear in this photograph. (Dr. David Nicolle collection)

A De Havilland Dove FR.Mk 3 – serial number 267 – of No. 3 Squadron, RIrAF, with a yellow camel painted on the red cheat line below the cockpit. The first of these aircraft reached Iraq in January 1948. (Albert Grandolini collection)

Table 2: RIrAF, Order of Battle, May 1948

Unit	Base	Equipment	Remarks
No. 1 Squadron	Mosul, Mafraq	Anson Mk I	CO Lieutenant Colonel Nadim Sadiq al-Ubaidi; in process of conversion to Fury FB.Mk 1
No. 3 Squadron	Rashid	M.57 Aerovan, Dove FR.Mk 3, Freighter C.Mk 31, AOP.5	Transport & liaison unit; including the Royal Flight
No. 4 Squadron	Kirkuk, Mafraq	Gladiator Mk II	CO Major Shams al-Din Abdallah
No. 7 Squadron	Rashid, Mafraq	Anson Mk I	CO Lieutenant Colonel Raouf Hassan; in the process of conversion to Fury FB.Mk 1
Flying School	Rashid	Tiger Moth, Nisr	

Colonel Muhammed Ra'uf Hassan. The Ansons of No. 1 Squadron RIrAF would also be sent to Mafraq though it is not clear when, some sources suggesting that No. 1 was sent when No. 7 was withdrawn to Iraq to be re-equipped with Hawker Furies.

What is clear is that Avro Ansons would form the backbone of the RIrAF's commitment to the Palestine War as bombers and perhaps more importantly in reconnaissance, using cameras installed in their noses. Some, and perhaps all, Iraqi Ansons based at Mafraq had their noses painted green – or, though less likely, blue – presumably to help Arab ground forces identify them as friendly.

The Gladiators of No. 4 Squadron under Major Shams al-Din Abdallah (CO from 1947 to 1951) were clearly sent to Mafraq before the Arab states officially entered the Palestine War, with their first operational sortie reportedly being on 20 March 1948. The last would be over a year later on 30 April 1949.

At some time during the Palestine War, two Miles M.57 Aerovans belonging to the Royal Iraqi Aero Society (civil registrations YI-ABV ex G-AJWK and YI-ABW) were commandeered as air ambulances to ferry casualties back to Baghdad. Whether they were unsuccessful in this role, as sometimes reported, remains unclear and there seem to be few reasons why Aerovans should have been unsuitable. Perhaps efforts were made to collect casualties from closer to the front lines and this proved impractical when Israeli air power increased or because the Israelis also used an Aerovan for similar purposes in June and July 1948.

Syrian Arab Air Force

Ongoing tensions between Syria and Turkey meant that the newly created SyAAF could not focus all of its limited resources

Table 3: SyAAF Aircraft availability, May 1948

Type	Role	Number available	Number operational
North American AT-6 Harvard	close support	17	12
Avro Anson	light bomber	1	1
Douglas C-47 Dakota	transport	3	3
Percival Proctor Mk. 5	communication	4	4
Fairchild F-24R Argus	communication and advanced training	5	5
Piper J-3C-65 Cub	communication and basic training	6	6
De Havilland DH82 Tiger Moth	basic training	6	6

on the Palestine conflict. The Iraqi government had also made clear its displeasure at Syria's rejection of a 'unity scheme' proposed by Baghdad, and by Syria's currently warm relations with Egypt and Saudi Arabia; both seen as rivals to Baghdad. Meanwhile the government in Damascus was aware that Transjordan's Hashemite ruler Abdullah Ibn Husayn, who had promoted himself from the rank of Amir to that of King on 25 May 1946, still harboured ambitions to rule a Greater Syria consisting of Transjordan, Syria, Palestine and Lebanon. Indeed, the military manoeuvres which took place in November 1947 seemed to envisage hostile threats from Zionist forces not only from the south-west but perhaps also from the south.

Information about the Syrian Air Force in any period is notoriously difficult to obtain but according to the available Israeli sources, the SyAAF's order of battle in May 1948 consisted of around 175 personnel, of whom between 40 and 50 were pilots (a surely inflated number), mostly very recently qualified. Of the available pilots, an estimated 33 to 35 were qualified to fly Harvards, the SyAAF's only combat aircraft (which were in reality armed trainers). Up to a dozen other men were reportedly available to fly liaison aircraft or Syria's handful of Dakotas. One Avro Anson may have been given or loaned to Syria by the REAF and two more would reportedly be loaned or given to Syria by the Iraqis during the conflict. The idea that Syria operated six Ansons around 1948–49 seems to stem from the fact that Iraqi Ansons would be active in the Syrian 'zone of operations,' operating from Mafraq in northern Transjordan, perhaps occasionally from Damascus, and sometimes attacking Israeli positions in Galilee from the direction of Syria. Thus, the SyAAF's order of battle in May 1948 is believed to have consisted of the aircraft as shown in Table 3.

Although British sources downgraded or dismissed a French role in the establishment of the Syrian Air Force, the SyAAF's structure was comparable to that of the *Armée de l'Air*. Its headquarters consisted of four divisions: administration (Division A), intelligence (Division B), operations and training (Division C), and general services (Division D). The primary operational air base was al-Mizzah outside Damascus where Harvards, Proctors, Arguses, Piper Cubs, Dakotas and the Anson were based. Another was west of Hama, both being commanded by officers with the rank of major who reported to a divisional commander. A third aerodrome at Dayr al-Zur in north-eastern Syria served as a reserve airbase while a fourth outside Homs served as the main depot and aircraft maintenance base, minor repairs being carried out at squadron level.

The SyAAF also already had, or would very soon establish, a presence at Establ in southern Lebanon, an ex-French airfield which lacked a hardened runway. The origins of the Syrian presence at Establ are obscure but it seems unlikely that the first cohort of Syrian student pilots trained there on ex-*Armée de l'Air* aeroplanes. In reality a SyAAF unit seems to have been sent to Establ to support Lebanese, Palestinian and Syrian troops on this front. It probably consisted of the second Harvard Flight to become operational, as suggested in the personal diary of a Harvard pilot, Lieutenant Faisal Nassif. In other words, at the start of the SyAAF's involvement in the Palestine War the only active combat aircraft were the Flight of 10 Harvards based at al-Mizzah outside Damascus.

It is also possible that the structure of the SyAAF was modified before it was committed to Palestine, Noam Hartoch suggesting that Syria's 12 operational Harvards were divided between Nos. 1 and 2 Squadrons, though only one was fully trained and operational by 15 May 1948. Each unit is understood to have included six pilots and six gunner-observers – just one crew for each available machine. Meanwhile No. 3 Squadron remained the largest unit in the SyAAF, though its aircraft were mostly light liaison and transport types, plus the Anson. In practice this probably meant that No. 3 Squadron

A Piper Cub of the Syrian Arab Air Force with aircrew and support personnel, sometime in 1948. (Albert Grandolini collection)

A T-6 Harvard/Texan of the Syrian Arab Air Force seen in June 1948 (see colour section for details). (Dr. David Nicolle collection)

was divided into two parts: the Anson Flight with as many as seven aircrew available, and the rest.

Recently, information has come to light concerning the appearance of SyAAF aircraft early in the Palestine War. For example, a Harvard with the Arabic name *Al-Anqa'a* (*Griffon*) on its engine cowling was photographed with SyAAF pilot Abd al-Karim Katma before taking off to attack an enemy position in June 1948. The aeroplane itself was painted in a relatively dark camouflage scheme with the name in white. Another Harvard had the name *Al-Sa'iqah* (*Lightning*) written in black on the other side of the engine cowling which had a lighter camouflage colour; this machine having been photographed at al-Mizzah around a similar date.

Operational control appears to have been a weak element during this, the SyAAF's first conflict, the evidence suggesting that SyAAF Headquarters at al-Mizzah retained such close control over combat sorties that Syrian and also Lebanese ground forces had limited influence over the selection of targets or tactics. According to Hartoch, each Army brigade had a communications officer responsible for radio communication with SyAAF HQ but these officers included Air Force pilots and navigators who sufficient understanding of what was required and was feasible.

In an effort to strengthen the recently created and inexperienced SyAAF, the Syrian government had insisted that the personnel and aeroplanes of Syrian Arab Airways be placed under Air Force control. However, the official decree was not counter-signed by the Syrian Army's General Staff until 12 May 1949, almost a year after the actual takeover. By then the three ex-Syrian Airways Dakotas were being used by the SyAAF, although plans to convert them into bombers had been dropped. Thus, the SyAAF's three Dakotas were only used as transports, nominally forming part of No. 3 Squadron.

A reliable roster of SyAAF aircrew is not available: the names of several men are known but do not include Captain Mahmud al-Rifa'i. Despite his combat experience in the *Luftwaffe*, he had instead joined the ALA The known SyAAF pilots and other aircrew who were Syrian citizens were therefore as follows:

Harvard aircrew:
Sergeant Muhi al-Din Attasi, No. 1 Squadron, gunner
Sergeant 1st Class Jaziri, No. 1 Squadron, pilot or gunner
Sergeant 1st Class Ghalib Faruqi, No. 1 Squadron, pilot or gunner
(rank unknown) Abd al-Karim Katma, probably No. 2 Squadron, pilot
2nd Lieutenant Khaidar, No. 2 Squadron, pilot
2nd Lieutenant Khani, No. 1 Squadron, pilot
2nd Lieutenant Ma'awat, No. 1 Squadron, pilot
Captain Azzam Maryud, No. 2 Squadron commander, pilot
2nd Lieutenant Muttia, No. 2 Squadron, pilot
Sergeant 1st Class Nabulsi, No. 1 Squadron, pilot or gunner
2nd Lieutenant Faisal Nassif, No. 1 Squadron, pilot
Sergeant 1st Class Ali Nat'ath, No. 1 Squadron, gunner
Sergeant 1st Class Natsri (Nazri?), No. 2 Squadron, gunner
Captain Sai'ah Sahil, squadron unknown, pilot (became a Dakota co-pilot after leaving the SyAAF)
Lieutenant Salim Sam'an, No. 1 Squadron or Reserve, pilot
Sergeant 1st Class Shwayk, No. 2 Squadron, pilot or gunner
Sergeant 1st Class Tinnawi, No. 1 Squadron, pilot or gunner
Lieutenant Umar Tzufar, No. 1 Squadron commander, pilot
Lieutenant Abdu Sa'id Wahaba, No. 2 Squadron, pilot or gunner (became a Syrian Arab Airways Dakota co-pilot after leaving the SyAAF)
2nd Lieutenant Zu'abi, No. 2 Squadron, pilot

C-47 Dakota and Anson aircrew:
Lieutenant Mamduh Azma, No. 3 Squadron commander, pilot
Lieutenant Gaylani, No. 3 Squadron, pilot
Lieutenant Kamal, No. 3 Squadron, pilot
Lieutenant Nasir, No. 3 Squadron, pilot
Lieutenant Al-Ns'asani, No. 3 Squadron, pilot

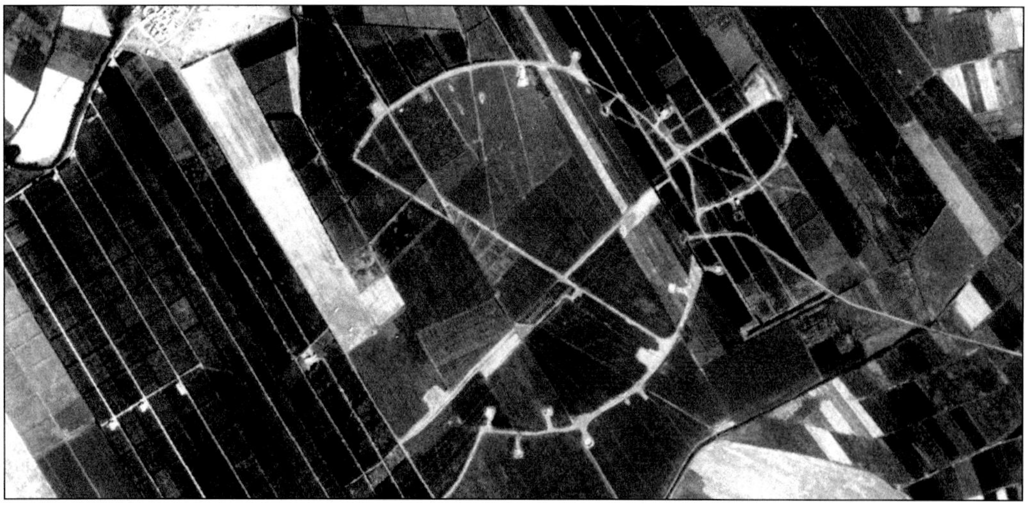

An aerial view of Istabl airfield, in Lebanon in the mid-1940s. (Dr. David Nicolle collection)

Table 4: SyAAF, Order of Battle, May 1948

Unit	Base	Equipment	Remarks
No. 1 Squadron	al-Mezzeh	Harvard/Texan	CO Lieutenant Umar Tzufar
No. 2 Squadron	Istabl	Harvard/Texan	CO Captain Azzam Maryud
No. 3 Squadron	al-Mezzeh	Cub, Anson, C-47/DC-3	CO Lieutenant Mamduh Azma

Lieutenant Shar'abi, No. 3 Squadron, pilot
Reserve or unspecified aircrew
2nd Lieutenant Sa'ad

Non-Syrian mercenaries had also been recruited to train Syrian personnel. The only reliable evidence of their taking part in combat missions involved Mato Dukovac while a Croatian wireless operator reportedly served as a navigator and bomb-aimer aboard an Avro Anson.

Although one flying training course had been completed before the SyAAF's commitment to the Palestine War, and a second would shortly do so, the Air Force command were fully aware that the training standards were at best only adequate. Meanwhile the number of pilots was so limited that losses could put the entire operation in peril. Furthermore Syria, like the other Arab states but unlike the new State of Israel, could not call upon large numbers of sympathetic airmen who had combat experience during the Second World War. There could be no Arab equivalent to the *Mahal* volunteers (or mercenaries, depending upon one's point of view) who formed the backbone of the Israeli Air Force throughout the Palestine War.

Of course, not all Syrian Air Force personnel were Muslim, any more than they were in the Egyptian or Iraqi Air Forces. For example, Lieutenant Abdu Sa'id Wahaba of No. 2 Squadron was a 25-year-old Christian. 2nd Lieutenant Faisal Nassif of No. 1 Squadron was Muslim but his newly married and recently pregnant wife Alice was from a Christian Syrian family, Nassif's diary showing that the young couple had to deal with occasionally tense relationships between their respective families.

OTHER AIR FORCES

The Saudi Arabian Air Force, insofar as it then existed, played no part in the Palestine War. The Transjordanian Arab Legion would commandeer two Arab Airways Dragon Rapides (TJ-AAC and TJ-AAP which later became RJAF serial numbers R300 and R301) but this may not have happened until 1949. Meanwhile, and perhaps more significantly, the British reinforced their presence at RAF Amman, after having abandoned their Palestine Mandate.

Israeli Air Force

On the other side of the conflict, the Israelis already had a significant number of aeroplanes, though no combat types, and the Arabs were fully aware that their foe possessed aircraft capable of dropping small bomb loads. Mainly used in close support of ground operations, approximately half were second-hand or older training and other light aircraft. The rest consisted of equally old transports, a few of which were equipped for bombing.

The Israeli *Sherut Avir*, forerunner of the Israeli Air Force, had taken over all the aerodromes, airfields and airstrips in Palestine with the exception of Ramat David, Haifa and one or more small landing grounds near Gaza and the Egyptian frontier. None had been damaged during the Second World War and the most important ones within areas already under Zionist control were fully operational and available to the *Sherut Avir*.

The Israelis therefore had four squadrons when fighting broke out between Arab and Israeli regular forces on 15 May 1948, the Galilee Squadron being based at Yavn'eel, the Tel Aviv Squadron at Sde Dov, and the Negev Squadron at Nir Am. The latter unit had only two aeroplanes but the total force included 28 light aircraft. A fourth unit, the 3rd Transport Squadron, was equipped with 18 heavy or medium transport aircraft, primarily to maintain an airlift between Europe and the newly proclaimed State of Israel.

The first three squadrons had made significant contributions to the Zionist fighting effort during the previous 'civil war' phases of the Palestine conflict, flying supplies to isolated areas, escorting convoys and evacuating wounded, while their bombing attacks and close support of ground forces had been crucial on several occasions. Nevertheless, there had been no Arab aircraft to oppose them and were undertaken under circumstances which made British intervention unlikely.

This force also had more than 1,000 personnel, including about 50 aircrew, a significant proportion of whom had combat experience during the Second World War. In addition to pilots currently training in Czechoslovakia, a substantial number of volunteer aircrew and groundcrew arrived in Palestine to fight for the Jewish state as soon as Israeli independence was declared. These were the famous *Mahal*, who came from the United Kingdom, South Africa, Canada and elsewhere. Most but not all were Jews, and English effectively became the official language of the new air force. Most also had administrative and planning experience – in some cases considerable such experience.

Furthermore, during the weeks leading up to the UN Truce of 11 June, the Israelis received shipments of artillery, mortars, tanks, and aeroplanes while also doubling their military manpower. Indeed, the Israeli Air Force would grow into a proper modern force during this first phase of fighting. Especially important was the Israeli Air Force's acquisition of a dozen Czechoslovakian Avia S-199s, licence-built Messerschmidt Bf 109s with licence-built Junkers Jumo engines. These were formed into a new fighter unit to be known as No. 101 Squadron and entered service at the rate of approximately one or two aeroplanes per day. They flew their first active mission on 29 May, though losing two machines and one pilot in the process.

NAVIES

The task allocated to the Egyptian Navy at the start of the conflict was to watch the Palestine coast. Further than this, both the Egyptian Navy and the newly created Israeli Navy were tasked with securing their own coasts and supporting friendly troops. Egypt therefore committed two minesweepers and five small transports to support the Egyptian Expeditionary Force as it advanced toward al-Majdal. The minesweepers had to operate at a significant distance, being based at Port Said, while the transports were normally moored off al-Arish which lacked an enclosed harbour. However, because of the continuing flow of Jewish immigrants into the new Jewish state, Egyptian naval forces began by bombarding Israeli harbours and coastal installations in an attempt to hinder the arrival of such immigrants. On 2 June, for example, an Egyptian minesweeper shelled Caesarea for 15 minutes, destroying harbour installations and sinking the only vessel present.

On the other side, several illegal immigrant ships seized by the Royal Navy had been interned in Haifa harbour. After these had been retaken on 22 April – without opposition from the British – Zionist technicians set about making repairs. After 15 May the British, who still controlled Haifa port and retained a naval base as part of the Haifa Enclave, allowed the Israelis to recondition their vessels in Haifa's shipyards. Although such work sped up and was now carried out openly, the British would not permit the arming of these ships, the arming of Israeli ships being undertaken at Tel Aviv. They included the former US Coast Guard cutter and some ex-British Royal Navy corvettes which thus formed a significant force. During the course of the conflict further ships would be acquired.

ARAB AND ISRAELI OBJECTIVES AS PRESENTED TO THE UN

Even as the Zionist settlers in Palestine declared their independence as the State of Israel on 14 May 1948, the struggle between Israelis and Arab Palestinians continued unabated, with local Arab militias generally getting the worst of such encounters. Then, as Arab regular forces crossed the frontiers into Palestine, the Secretary-General of the Arab League sent a cablegram dated 15 May to the United Nations, stating the reasons which had prompted the Arab states to intervene militarily. After tracing the history of the Palestine question in some detail, this cable set out the Arab League's justification for armed intervention. In fact, the Secretary-General of the Arab League did not consider the Arab countries to be at war in the full sense. He regarded the Arab intervention as being a police operation to protect Palestinian Arabs from Zionist attacks. Furthermore, he maintained that the Arab League was merely taking over from the British who had failed to maintain peace in the Holy Land.

An Egyptian reconnaissance photograph of Kibbutz Negba, probably taken by one of the modified REAF Spitfire F.Mk 9s before the Palestine War, during their clandestine sorties over Palestine in early May 1948. (Dr. David Nicolle collection)

Israel also turned to the UN Security Council for help and here Trygve Lee, the first Secretary-General of the United Nations (2 February 1946 to 10 November 1952), agreed with the Israeli accusation that the Arabs had launched an aggression which violated the UN Charter. He therefore urged the Security Council and the key members of the UN to take 'necessary measures,' including sanctions against the Arab states which were involved in this military intervention.

THE BRITISH POSITION

Meanwhile the British seemed more concerned about restrictions which the Egyptian government wanted to put upon the RAF's ability to fly over Egyptian territory, as the British air attaché later explained in his first report on the REAF;

> A state of Martial Law had been proclaimed and Egyptian 'Notices to Airmen' were issued which imposed severe restrictions upon day flying, declared several prohibited areas including Suez, which made it difficult for the Royal Air Force to use the bombing range in that area, and placed a total ban on night flying over all Egypt.

Following representations by the air attaché to the Egyptian Ministry of War, discussions took place which resulted in almost complete clearance for day flying and for use of the bombing range near Suez. Some limitations nevertheless remained concerning flight paths and night flying, and;

> To obtain these concessions, particularly as regards night flying, the Egyptians were given on loan, the temporary use of an early warning radar set to be operated in close liaison with the Royal Air Force operated equipment so that the Egyptians could check the presence of aircraft in the agreed area where Royal Air Force flying training was to take place.

Nevertheless, British pilots still had to be very careful, particularly near Suez, because Egyptian anti-aircraft gunners were liable to open fire at any aircraft they suspected of being Israeli or which they could not immediately confirm was friendly. Even so, it seems surprising that the Egyptian government should have allowed such freedom to the RAF during a time of active hostilities.

STRATEGIES

Egyptian Army

Whatever the Secretary-General of the Arab League might have expected, the first phase of the 'official' Palestine War promptly took on the character of a conventional war in what would prove to be the most critical four weeks of the entire conflict. Although the Israelis had a greater number of troops in the field at the time, it was marked by Arab successes on all fronts. Even so, these were notably less than Arab leaders had anticipated. Some have claimed

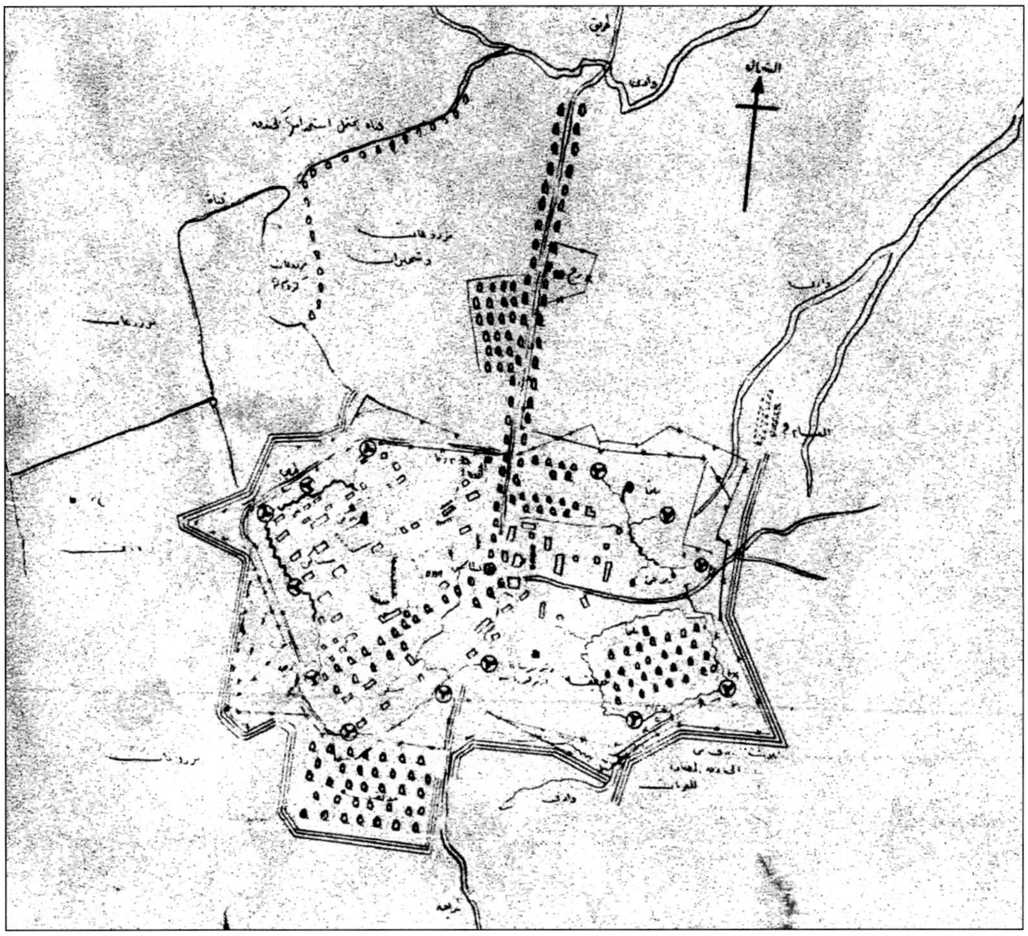

A detailed sketch of Kibbutz Negba and its defences, prepared on the basis of REAF reconnaissance. (Dr. David Nicolle collection)

that outright victory would have been within the reach of Arab armies if they had coordinated their battle plans and pursued them with determination. This remains a matter of opinion, but during this first phase 19 identifiable 'battles' were fought. In most of them the Arab armies had the initiative and succeeded in taking control of most of the territory allotted to the proposed Arab State of Palestine under the Partition Plan. The Arab Legion also placed part of Jerusalem under siege while the Egyptian Army cut the Negev off from other Israeli-held territory. What these armies failed to do was destroy Israeli fighting strength.

Egyptian strategy resulted in Egyptian forces being split into two almost independent groups. The larger was the western force moving along the Mediterranean, forming a narrow, wedge-like front which thrust towards Tel Aviv. South and east of this threatening wedge, the Egyptian front would broaden as it faced a strong Israeli defensive position at Kibbutz Negba. The front then swept east toward hills around Hebron. Its eastern part was held by few and scattered Egyptian units, meaning that the isolation of Israeli forces in the Negev never became complete. Small Israeli units from the north would rarely have much difficulty infiltrating through this part of the Egyptian front to reinforce their comrades in the Negev.

Meanwhile a second Egyptian force, the so-called Light Force, would soon be positioned in the northern part of the Hebron Hills, threatening another important Israeli defensive location at Kibbutz Ramat Rahel. In this area Egyptian positions would loosely overlap the left flank of the Arab Legion's front while local Palestinian Arab militia units theoretically plugged gaps between Egyptian and Legion position in the area of Latrun.

Egyptian soldiers inside one of the ex-British 'police forts' in Palestine. Although this photograph is almost certainly staged for the camera, several of these concrete fortresses played a major role during the Palestine War. (Dr. David Nicolle collection)

Haydar Pasha, the Egyptian Minister of Defence, with Egyptian Army officers, discussing planning in front of a large map of Palestine. (Dr. David Nicolle collection)

A Douglas C-47 Dakota of the REAF in flight to or from al-Arish during the Palestine War. This appears to be one of the aircraft which were only used as transports and retained their overall bare metal finish. (Dr. David Nicolle collection)

Within southern Palestine, which would soon become the Egyptians' theatre of operations, the strategic village of Falujah was currently held by Muslim Brotherhood irregulars under Egyptian officers. In the same area, a formidable police fort overlooked a strategically important crossroads next to the village of Iraq Suwaidan. It had been taken over by a Muslim Brotherhood force when the British departed. Elsewhere in southern Palestine the situation remained fluid until regular Egyptian troops arrived to defend the surviving Palestinian Arab areas and establish some sort of front.

For its part, the *Haganah* had established a link with the south by seizing control of the 'middle road' from Julis to Burair, plus the villages of Kaukaba and Hulaiqat. Their inhabitants were expelled and most sought refuge in Falujah. Here it worth noting that Egyptian sources often referred to Israeli settlements by the name of the nearest Palestinian Arab village. Those of the latter which lay within the battle area would be, or had already been, demolished and their populations expelled as refugees to surrounding areas or neighbouring Arab states. Furthermore, these villages no longer appear on normal maps of Israel so the historian has to rely on earlier, usually British military surveys.

REAF

During the Palestine War it was the Royal Egyptian Air Force that carried out by far the greater proportion of Arab air actions. The tactics used in support of ground troops and in searching for the newly formed Israel Defence Force/Air Force were based upon the RAF's *Land/Air Warfare Pamphlet No. 1 Air Support Command.* From 15–19 May 1948, the REAF primarily focused upon gaining air control and destroying Israeli aeroplanes while also providing direct support and air reconnaissance to Egyptian Army units as they advanced into Palestine. The primary role of the REAF then changed and from 19–22 May its main aim was to destroy or render unusable the port of Tel Aviv, along with Israeli military production sites and transport systems. Of course, the REAF also sought to maintain its dominance while directly assisting the Egyptian Army and carrying out reconnaissance.

To some extent the two lines of the Egyptian thrust into Palestine were reflected in the tasks allocated to the REAF. According to Major Muhammad Kamil Siddiq's article *Air War in Palestine*, written in October 1948 before the Palestine War ended, the REAF nominally operated on two fronts like the Egyptian Army. One supported the Egyptian Army while the other supported the Transjordanian Arab Legion and those elements of the Egyptian Light Force fighting alongside the Legion. The work of reconnaissance, taking aerial photographs of Tel Aviv, its aerodromes, other aerodromes further north, and fortified settlements closer to the front, was an almost separate issue. At the same time the REAF flew patrols over the eastern Mediterranean, searching for ships heading for Tel Aviv and Haifa.

A few months after the Palestine War ended, an article – probably written by the CO of the REAF – focused on the role of the REAF's multi-engine aeroplanes. In addition to supporting the army in the field as transports, they targeted communications centres, factories, fuel dumps and aerodromes using high explosive and incendiary bombs. The writer referred to cases where Egyptian bombers, operating at night, followed Israeli aeroplanes to their airfields, the lights of which were only switched on to enable an Israeli machine to land before being turned off again. Egyptian machines then attacked the enemy aerodrome while the landing lights were still on or had just been turned off. The success or otherwise of such attempts remains unknown.

The REAF's larger aircraft, by which the CO of the REAF meant its Douglas C-47 Dakotas and Curtiss C-46 Commandos, carried military supplies and almost certainly some personnel to Transjordan. There were similar communications flights between Cairo and Damascus and Beirut. Nevertheless, the bulk of such flights were between Almaza and al-Arish.

A further account of the role of the REAF written by the British air attaché a couple of years later, also focused on the role of the transport squadron. He wrote that;

> The work of the aircraft would therefore involve aerial transport, carrying men and their equipment, and carrying out battlefield support. This led to a dispersal of effort, particularly by the long-range aircraft. As to why the Air Force's aircraft were not all put into one task, it would seem that the Egyptian technicians were hampered by their lack of spares and the need to put all they had into modifying transport aircraft into bombers.

For the REAF Tactical Air Force based at al-Arish aerodrome, tactical and strategic missions were barely differentiated, almost everything being at relatively short range. They, unlike their Syrian and the Iraqi colleagues, were nevertheless in a position to attack strategic targets. Nevertheless, most sorties were to provide direct air support to Egyptian and Transjordanian ground troops, attacking fortified enemy settlements prior to a ground attack or harassing Israeli troops wherever they were found. Supply convoys to fortified settlements in the Negev were a further target, along with a determined effort to undermine Israeli morale in Tel Aviv and even Haifa by attacking the harbour and its warehouses, communications hubs and nearby factories. Only later, as the tide of war turned against the Arab states, would the REAF have to construct dispersal airfields within Sinai and also fly supply-dropping missions to the besieged Egyptian garrison at Falujah.

Personnel of the REAF's Tactical Air Force listening to a Muslim imam at al-Arish in 1948. (Abu Zaid family archive)

The anonymous author of the semi-official *Bab al-Sadis*, referred to units which flew offensive operations from Almaza outside Cairo as 'the Strategic Air Force.' This grandiose name for a handful of multi-engine aeroplanes and their crews reflected the REAF's ambitions during the Palestine conflict. These raids began shortly after the start of the 'official' war and would increase with the arrival of additional aeroplanes. Their initial tasks were to render a number of aerodromes and airfields in southern and central Palestine unusable, even though some were not yet actually being used by the enemy; such targets including Aqir, Lydda, Petah Tikva and Bayt Daras in the hope that the Israelis would have to rely solely on airfields which lacked hardened runways. This was to help the Tactical Air Force maintain air superiority and hopefully also prevent the enemy providing direct air support to his own troops.

Attacks on aerodromes further north were intended to inhibit the enemy's use of his longer-range aircraft against Egyptian targets. Finally, it was hoped that sorties by the so-called Strategic Air Force at Almaza could continue the work of the Tactical Air Force at al-Arish against enemy communications centres and assembly areas. According to *Bab al-Sadis*, the Strategic Air Force eventually undertook some 26 such missions, dropping about 136,000kg (300,000lbs) of high explosive and incendiary bombs for the loss of two aircrew. Unfortunately, nothing comparable to the Operational Diary of Tactical Air Force Operations at al-Arish is yet available for the Strategic Air Force at Almaza, so the date and location of the loss of two aircrew are unknown. Maybe they were from the second Dakota which the Israelis claimed to have shot down over Tel Aviv and which is emphatically denied by the REAF. Most likely they were the crew of a Short Stirling bomber lost in a training accident.

The work of the Tactical Air Force intensified before the First UN Truce came into effect, its main targets remaining a line of fortified settlements north and east of the strategic Iraq Suwaidan crossroads which became the Israeli front-line following the loss of Nizzanim on 7 June.

The British still maintained that access to RAF supplies within Egypt – meaning the official transfer of such material rather than the pilfering of spares from British supply dumps – remained essential to REAF operations. The British thus believed they retained some control over the REAF. On 29 May an arms embargo came into effect, followed at the start of June by the British halting all sales of military equipment, including material already allocated to the REAF at the RAF's No. 107 Maintenance Unit at Kasfarit which was now placed under lock and key.

Iraq

Early in May 1948, the Iraqi contingent had deployed between Irbid and the Jordan River where it prepared to cross the river and capture the Zionist settlement of Gesher. So, to make the crossing difficult for Iraqi troops, the Israelis blew up the Majama Bridge facing Gesher. In addition to supporting Iraqi ground forces in Palestine, both directly and with some form of communications sorties, the RIrAF would also attack some strategic targets in the central part of the coastal plain between Tel Aviv and Haifa. Although such tasks overlapped areas nominally allocated to the Egyptians or Syrians, there appears to have been very little coordination between the three Arab air forces. Meanwhile, the RIrAF had to provide air support to the Arab Legion because Transjordan had no air force of its own.

Syria

The situation which the Syrian Army faced when it crossed the Palestinian front in May 1948 bore virtually no resemblance to its recent manoeuvres in southern Syria. Rather than defending their capital against an enemy attack, the Syrians were now on the offensive in Galilee, if only tentatively. The SyAAF was thus expected to give close support to Syrian ground forces while attacking enemy targets within range. Although the Syrians lacked aircraft for an air superiority role, SyAAF's Harvards would be used to find and destroy enemy aircraft on the ground. Where sorties in direct support of Syrian ground forces were concerned, the men on the ground seem to have been given greater responsibility for target selection than was seen on other Arab fronts. The same seems to have been the case when it came to assessing the effectiveness of resulting SyAAF air operations.

Even at this early stage, the Syrian High Command in Damascus already feared the possibility of Israeli air attacks upon the Syrian capital; perhaps even a ground assault in the same direction. In fact, despite the SyAAF's lack of experience, the Syrians apparently had a more realistic understanding of the threat they might face if the campaign dragged on for more than a few weeks. In the event, after the first and second phases of the Palestine War, operations by the SyAAF were sporadic, almost always in reaction to an Israeli action, and had limited impact.

Transjordan

In April 1948, when King Abdullah decided to intervene in Palestine, he hoped to avoid fighting Israeli forces. His only concern, as agreed between Transjordanian Prime Minister Tawfiq Abu al-Huda Pasha and the British Secretary of State for Foreign Affairs Ernest Bevin, was to occupy the Arab part of partitioned Palestine as a step towards merging that area with his kingdom. However, the smooth occupation King Abdullah and Glubb Pasha, the King's most senior military commander, hoped for turned into severe fighting because of Israeli moves to occupy Jerusalem.

3

FIRST PHASE (15 MAY–11 JUNE 1948), DAY BY DAY

At 22.00 hrs local time on 14 May 1948, the command centres of the Egyptian Army, the Egyptian Navy and the REAF received a message, telling them to expect a signal from the King and to act upon it immediately. The code word indicating immediate action would be 'Ibrahim'. More detailed orders sent to the REAF earlier that day confirmed that its role was to provide close support to the Army and Navy, transport personnel to the front, and evacuate casualties. It was considered impractical to attempt more because of the REAF's acute shortage of spare parts.

To the north-east, the only Arab forces currently in Jerusalem were some elements of the ALA plus GMA irregulars without proper organisation or overall leadership. The Arab Legion units which were under British control, had similarly evacuated the country. Meanwhile, four Legion regiments were due to enter Palestine the following day and had camped on the other side of the Jordan. This absence of a significant Arab force in Jerusalem presented the Israelis with an irresistible temptation to seize the Holy City which had been supposed to remain an international zone, separate from the Jewish and Arab states. The *Haganah* command therefore committed two contingents to clear the Arab part of the city plus the Shaikh Jarrah quarter to the north, and to establish contact with Zionist – now Israeli – strongpoints on Mount Scopus. Israeli forces also occupied the railway station, in an area known as the German Colony, as well as an ex-British barracks.

In the face of these moves Arab irregulars retreated into the walled Old City and closed its gates. The Old City was itself divided into four quarters, the largest being those on the north which were mainly inhabited by Muslims and Christians respectively. In the southwestern corner was the Armenian Quarter, to the east of which lay the Jewish Quarter, long inhabited by religious Jews and currently having around 1,700 inhabitants. During the last days of the Mandate, over 300 trained *Haganah* and *Etzel* troops had entered this Jewish Quarter to consolidate the inhabitants' resistance and to raise their morale.

Due to Israeli pressure on the Old City, the Palestinians now appealed to King Abdullah, but General Glubb, operating within the limits agreed between Ernest Bevin and Tawfiq Abu al-Huda, opposed any Arab Legion involvement in Jerusalem. Instead Glubb hoped to establish a truce in the city and tried to convince

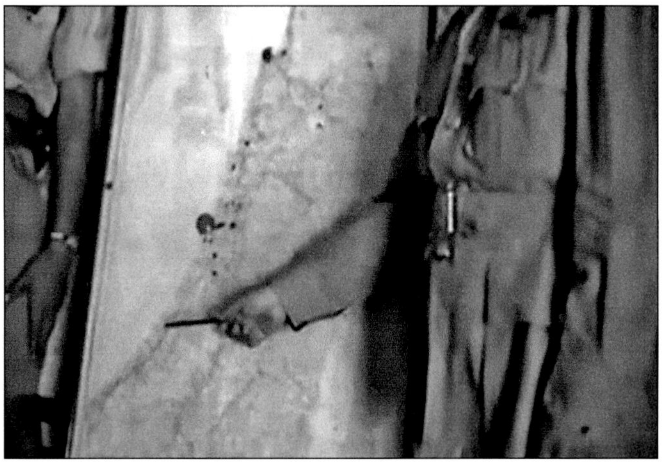

A REAF officer pointing to a wall-map in the briefing room at al-Arish aerodrome during the early part of the Palestine War. He appears to be pointing at the major fortified Israeli settlement of Yad Mordechai (Dayr Sunayd). Enemy-held aerodromes were indicated on the map by dark dots. (Dr. David Nicolle collection)

Troops of the Arab Legion in the Old City of Jerusalem in 1948. (Dr. David Nicolle collection)

the King that Jerusalem would swallow half his forces, resulting in the Legion being unable to hold the rest of what became the West Bank. Furthermore, Jerusalem would thereby be outflanked and lost. Meanwhile the UN Truce Committee (UNTC) informed King Abdullah that they hoped to progress with a truce the following day. Abdullah therefore agreed to wait.

By 14 May, the Syrian 1st Brigade under Colonel Abd al-Wahab al-Hakim was in southern Lebanon, ready to advance towards Safad. But under King Abdullah's new directive as nominal overall commander of the Arab military intervention, this Syrian brigade had to return to Syria, to adopt a new course for a new mission. Al-Hakim therefore moved across the Golan Heights towards Samakh, south of Lake Tiberias. Here he was to occupy the village and establish a bridgehead across the Jordan. The Israelis had expected the main Syrian thrust to be north of Lake Tiberias, so only the second mobile battalion of the Golani Brigade, the settlers themselves, plus some other elements, were in position to slow a Syrian advance south of the Lake until reinforcements could arrive. During the night of 14–15 May, in an attempt to halt a feared Lebanese advance into the Finger of Galilee, an Israeli battalion occupied two more Arab villages; Qadas (Kedesh, which was unusual in having a largely Shi'a Muslim population), and al-Malkiyah.

15 MAY 1948

Ground Operations

On 15 May 1948, precisely as the British Mandate came to an end, the Arab League put into effect its resolution of 12 April aimed at ensuring Palestine for its Arab inhabitants. Early in the day, the Arab forces began to enter Palestine. In the north a Lebanese force responded to new directives from King Abdullah and advanced towards al-Malkiyah to link up with ALA units in this area while Syrian units advanced moved towards Samakh, south of Lake Tiberias.

On the central front, Arab Legion units crossed the Jordan to take up positions in Jinin, Nablus, and Ramallah. However, the Israeli offensive in Jerusalem led to some Arab Legion units being withdrawn from Nablus to defend the Holy City and its surroundings. This in turn meant that Iraqi troops were sent to Nablus, Jinin and Tulkarm while Iraqi engineers established a pontoon bridge to replace the demolished bridge over the Jordan. This they did under cover of artillery and mortar fire while Iraqi infantry, who forded the Jordan River, occupied a stronghold north of Gesher and the village of al-Majama east of the Jewish settlement. As soon as the pontoon bridge was completed, the Iraqi armoured battalion moved to the west bank, south of the settlement.

The Israelis remained largely on the defensive, relying on well-fortified settlements in key positions to halt Arab forces. From these locations they would also be able to threaten Arab lines of

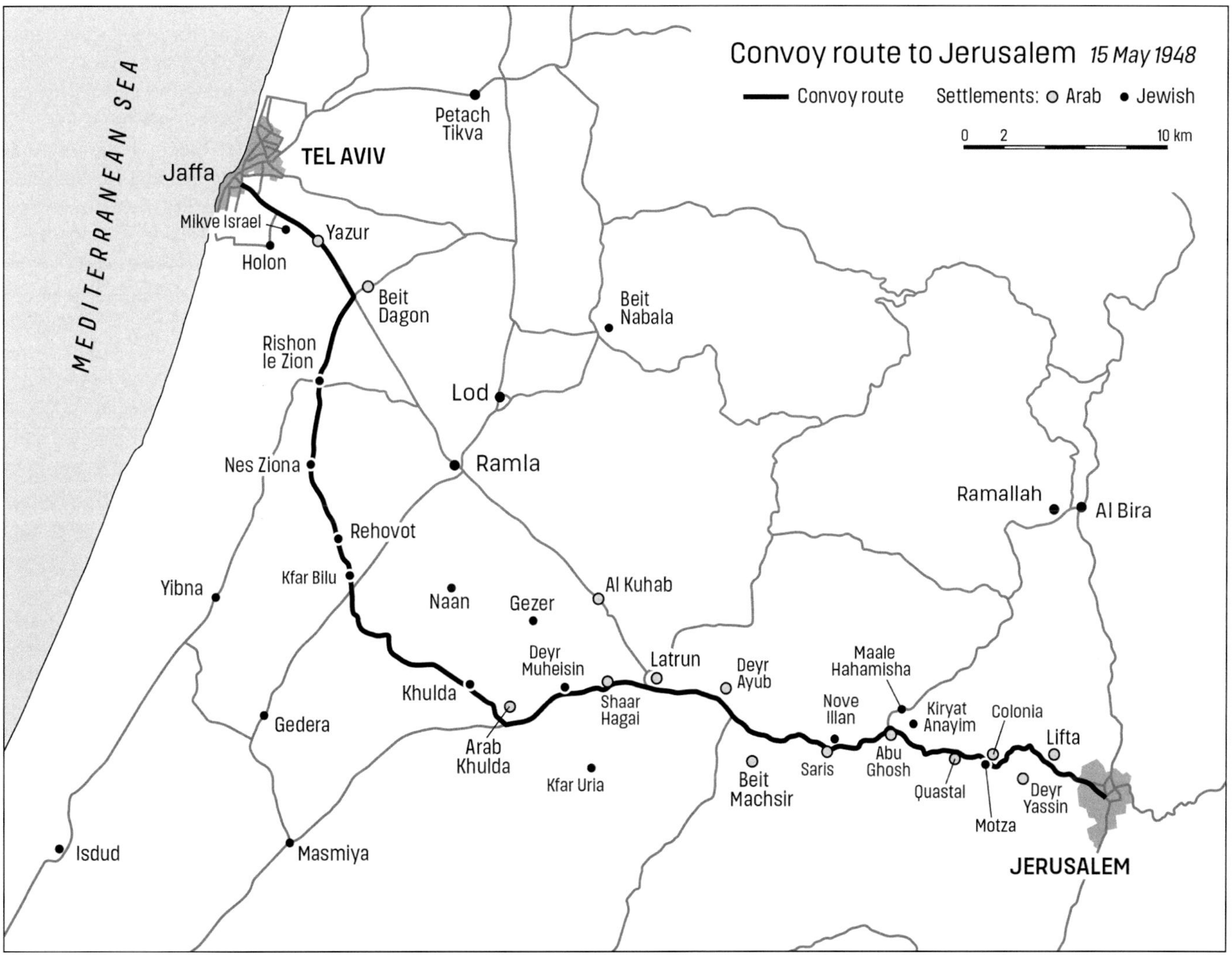

The situation along the road connecting Tel Aviv with Jerusalem as of 15 May 1948. (Map by Paul Hewitt)

An armoured car of the Egyptian Army in southern Palestine. (Dr. David Nicolle collection)

communications. Meanwhile, they feverishly built up, equipped and reorganised their own armed forces.

Having set off early in the morning of 15 May, the Egyptian Army's first objective was to secure Gaza and Beersheba, General al-Muwawi fearing that Gaza might be seized by Israeli troops or at least be raided from nearby Israeli settlements. This main Egyptian force consisted of around 5,000 troops in a brigade group led by al-Muwawi himself. The Egyptian southern thrust crossed the frontier at al-Auja and pushed east towards Beersheba. Meanwhile the first elements of the Egyptian Light Force under Lieutenant Colonel Ahmad Abd al-Aziz, having entered Palestine on 6 May, were busy blocking roads between the coastal plain and the Negev.

On the other side, the *Haganah* high command attempted to block the southern routes into Palestine, using fortified Zionist settlements located in strong tactical positions which dominated their surrounding areas. These were to resist the enemy's attack while threatening their flanks and communication. In addition, the Negev and Givati Brigades were deployed to confront the Egyptian advance. The Negev Brigade (about 2,000 troops) was commanded by Colonel Nahum Sarig, its role being to defend the area between al-Majdal and Bayt Jibrin, west and northwest of Beersheba, and south of the lateral road. The Givati Brigade (3,299 troops) commanded by Colonel Shimon Avidan was to defend the area immediately north of the lateral road. These two brigades were also to consolidate the settlements in their respective areas and launch counterattacks whenever the Egyptian thrust weakened.

The ultimate task of the Egyptian coastal thrust was to take Tel Aviv but many Israeli settlements along this route first needed to be secured. A detachment of infantry supported by artillery was therefore ordered to take the settlement and airstrip at Nir Am which, lying 15km from the international frontier, was home to the Israeli Air Force's Negev Squadron. But while the main Egyptian force quickly reached Khan Yunis and took over from the local Palestinian militia, such fierce resistance was encountered at Nir Am that the Egyptian assault was abandoned, a detachment of irregulars being left to contain the settlement while the main Egyptian force moved on.

Elsewhere another attempt was made by Muslim Brotherhood volunteers to take the Israeli settlement of Kfar Darom, this time supported by three Egyptian tanks. The latter were, however, forced back by the settlement's single anti-tank weapon and the Muslim Brotherhood volunteers suffered heavy casualties as they attempted to press their assault. So, Kfar Darom was also bypassed while the irregulars were left behind to contain it, such setbacks doing nothing to improve relations between the Muslim Brotherhood and the Egyptian Army. Another reason why the Egyptian advance into Palestine bypassed several Israeli fortified settlements was to save ammunition, along with a belief that the Israelis would evacuate these places if they were cut off. Furthermore, the Egyptian military command wanted to press ahead towards more important objectives, the principal Arab town of Gaza being reached at 1900 hrs on 16 May.

To the south, the second Egyptian force occupied the border police post at al-Auja and headed northwards towards Beersheba and Hebron, in order to link with elements of the Arab Legion south of Jerusalem. From here they would move against Ramat Rahel, which was the southernmost point held by the Israelis in the area of New Jerusalem (as distinct from the Old City and its eastern suburbs).

During the morning, two Jordanian Brigades crossed the Allenby Bridge into Palestine, followed by a garrison force consisting of the 6th Battalion. The 1st Brigade (1st and 3rd Regiments) was sent to Nablus while the 3rd Brigade (2nd and 4th Regiments) was to concentrate at Ramallah. Meanwhile the 6th Battalion would be divided between Jericho and al-Jiftlik. In fact, the Arab Legionnaires were the first of the Arab armies to see significant action. Having crossed the Jordan, an Arab Legion force moved towards Jerusalem where the garrison of the Jewish Quarter now numbered 200 *Haganah* and 100 *Irgun*, plus around 1,200 others. There the Arab Legion halted, awaiting the outcome of negotiations conducted by UN officials. Throughout 15–16 May, the UNTC struggled unsuccessfully to establish a ceasefire while *Haganah* and *Etzel* forces increased their pressure on the Old City. Although the Israeli provisional government backed these attacks, it refused to accept responsibility for a clear Jewish aggression which, they alleged, was being carried out by dissident groups of *Irgun tzeva'i l'eumi* (*Etzel*) and *Lohamei Herut Yisrael* (*Lehi*). By 16 May, before Arab regular armies reached the Jerusalem area, Jewish forces had taken control of most districts outside the fortified walls of the Old City, except those directly to the east. As a result, most of the proposed Internationalized Zone was occupied by Israeli forces.

Elsewhere, according to a Transjordan Defence Ministry communique transcribed by the BBC Monitoring at 1300 hrs GMT on 16 May; 'Lydda airport was occupied yesterday [on the 15th] and the Transjordan Army's reinforcements [were] sent there [on the 16th?]. The Kalenzia [Qalandiya] colony was also occupied yesterday. It is situated on the Ramallah-Jerusalem road near Qalandiya airfield'.

In the north, at one hour after midnight on 14–15 May and before the arrival of his heavy weapons, Colonel al-Hakim crossed the Palestine frontier with two Syrian Army infantry battalions. Having just moved from southern Lebanon to a new launch position, this force was tired and so al-Hakim decided not to stop until daylight while occupying Tal al-Qasr, southeast of Lake Tiberias. His men also exchanged fire with Israeli forces south of Lake Tiberias. Then on 15 May Colonel al-Hakim sent three detachments to attack Samakh and two other settlements, Massada and Shaar Hagolan, which lay to his south.

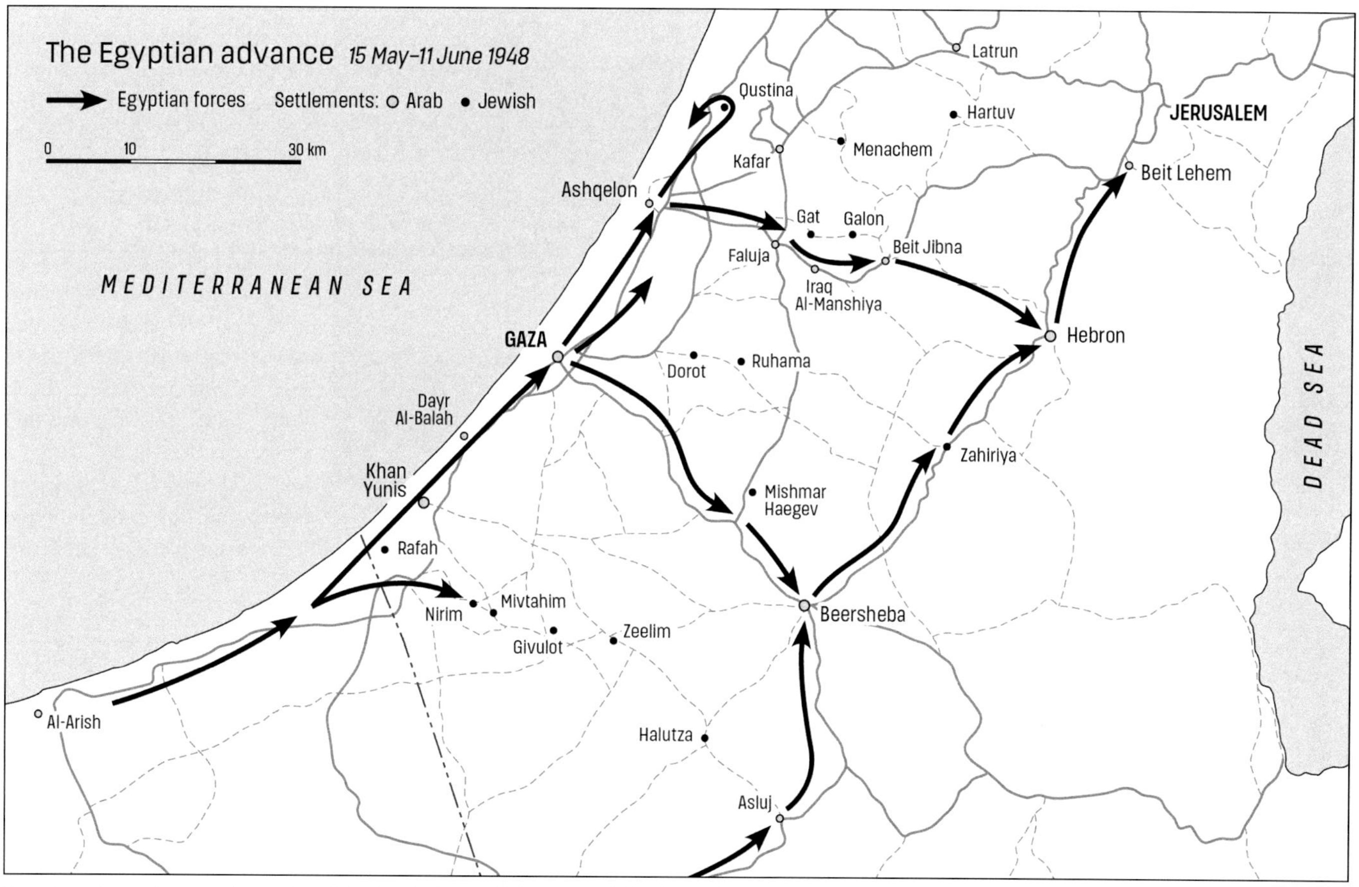

Egyptian advance into south-western Palestine, 15 May – 11 June 1948. (Map by Paul Hewitt)

The gunner of a REAF Westland Lysander, reportedly photographed in 1948. (REAF Museum)

Egyptian Air Operations

During the first hour of the morning, or at 0100 hrs, the codeword 'Ibrahim' was transmitted to all Egyptian forces, including the REAF at al-Arish. An hour later the Egyptian Spitfires were ready to go. A further message from headquarters asked if the machines were ready, while other messages were sent to units, squadrons, apparently even to individual pilots and air technicians, concluding with the statement; 'I am telling you "Ibrahim" – are you willing and are you ready? So, get on with it!'

Headquarters also confirmed that the main target would be Tel Aviv aerodrome (Sde Dov) with secondary targets being Kfar Darom between Gaza and Khan Yunis, Aqir aerodrome and Israeli settlements outside Bayt Hanun and at Be'erot Yitzhak ('old' Be'erot Yitzhak, now called Alumim). This time the messages concluding with the words 'Good luck, Headquarters.' The first raids actually took off from al-Arish just before dawn which was at approximately 0440 hrs, and the aircraft remained in the vicinity of the airfield until all were airborne, whereupon they split into Flights which headed for their designated targets.

Despite the lack of available Operational Diary pages for 15 May, a great deal of information is available about this largely successful day. Fourteen numbered missions were flown from al-Arish, almost all by more than one aircraft, a total of 48 aircraft taking to the air although not all these flights were operational. Of the 11 fighter missions by the REAF's Spitfire 9s, only four were operational, providing air cover for other aeroplanes. Some were presumably to protect al-Arish aerodrome, though the fact that four were flown by Hurricanes suggests they included reconnaissance sorties. No fighter sorties were flown by Spitfire Vs. Spitfire 9s also flew eight or nine fighter-bomber sorties while Spitfire Vs flew eight. Two reconnaissance missions were flown by Lysanders from al-Arish, while four bombing missions were flown by Dakotas. Dakotas also flew four communications or transport missions, as did the REAF's Doves, along with two communications flights by Ansons, all of which were from Cairo, probably from Almaza.

There were meanwhile 29 sorties from Almaza on 15 May, probably training or communications flights though those described as fighter missions might have included flights over Cairo to reassure the inhabitants. They consisted of nine flights by Spitfire 9s and four by Hurricanes. Those from Almaza which were described as fighter-bomber missions were presumably also training; there being eight by Spitfire Vs on this day. This may also have been the case with the four 'bombing missions by transport aircraft' undertaken by Dakotas. Flights from Hilwan were clearly specified as being training, there being four such fighter sorties by Spitfire 9s and just one such fighter-bomber sortie, again by a Spitfire 9.

The aerodrome of Sde Dov was the Israeli air arm's primary base and lay next to the coast on the northern edge of Tel Aviv. It was

An aerial view of Ramat David Air Base in early 1949. (Dr. David Nicolle collection)

Later that morning the Egyptians released an official communique stating; 'Our aircraft raided the Tel Aviv area and hit the port facilities and the industrial area on the eastern side of the city. Our aircraft also raided Kfar Darom, Aqir, Bayt Hanun and [old] Be'erot Yitzhak and all our aircraft returned safely.' There was no mention of an attack upon Sde Dov aerodrome where the REAF did suffer a loss. According to a subsequent, overoptimistic communique issued by the Egyptian Ministry of Defence and broadcast by Cairo Radio at 2215;

> Our bombers completely destroyed Petah Tivka airport [Kfar Sirkin airfield, previously RAF Petah Tikva]. They also raided Aqir airport and damaged two aeroplanes [on the ground]. Several ships carrying war equipment have been seen heading for Tel Aviv harbour. The Egyptian Royal Air Force raided Tel Aviv harbour at 1030, our bombers dropping high explosives on the docks. The quay collapsed into the sea. At 1350 the harbour was again raided and warehouses were destroyed. At 1600 high explosives and incendiary bombs were again dropped, blasting and setting afire transit stores. The fires could be seen ten miles away. All our planes returned safely. Our losses were negligible compared to the scope of the operations.

An unidentified REAF pilot dismounting from his Spitfire at al-Arish. This photograph was published in the newspaper *al-Ahram*, early during the Palestine War. (Dr. David Nicolle collection)

the most significant target on this first day of REAF action, these attacks being led by *Qa'id Asrab* Muhamad Abd al-Hamid Abu Zaid. There is also evidence that it was amongst the first to be struck. Sde Dov would, however, also be where the REAF suffered its first operational loss.

The latter sentence was the first indication that the REAF had lost anything at all.

Early accounts by both sides concerning the attacks on Sde Dov aerodrome were exaggerated and misleading. Over the years these were moderated, but the REAF's biography of *Qa'id Asrab* Muhammad Abu Zaid claimed that on 15 May he had destroyed a Dakota as it was landing – in fact it was preparing to take-off – and had set hangers on fire. One of the first Israeli accounts of this raid merely stated that three Egyptian Spitfires approached Tel Aviv from the sea and flew towards Reading Power Station, beyond which was Tel Aviv (Sde Dov) airfield. They then dropped bombs from 300m before turning back towards the sea. A fuller and more accurate Israeli account later stated that on the morning of the 15th, at around 0500, two REAF Spitfires came in low over the Mediterranean, roared over the Yarkon river at 300m then dived on Reading Power Station which stood between the airfield and harbour. One circled above while the other dropped two 250lb (113kg)

Probably one of earliest photographs of Barakat's Spitfire F/LF.Mk 9 that force-landed on Herzliya beach, with its nose in the water. (Dr. David Nicolle collection)

Barakat's Spitfire F/LF.Mk 9 on the beach north of Tel Aviv with its left wing missing. (Dr. David Nicolle collection)

Another view of the same aircraft with the left wing missing. The Israeli in the foreground is studying the probable camera mount. (Dr. David Nicolle collection)

bombs causing slight damage to the power station. Both then strafed the area two or three times.

A radio broadcast from Beirut at 1200 on 15 May and based upon the official Egyptian version of events, added that; 'The colour of the smoke and flames [when the harbour area was bombed] showed that ammunition stores were hit. Thirty-four planes participated in the raid [an exaggeration even if all the sorties from al-Arish are taken into account].... One bomb fell outside the harbour area, killing one person.'

These accounts would soon be elaborated, not least by an American newspaper reporter working for *Time* magazine. He claimed to have been standing on Tel Aviv's corniche when an air-raid alarm signalled the approach of hostile aircraft. This supposedly consisted of a single machine at high altitude which looked so unthreatening that people stopped to stare at it, joking that it would fall into the water. The plane then swooped so low that someone joked that the pilot wanted to place his bombs on target by hand. The low level of such attacks would be emphasised by the Commander of the REAF in an article published on 1 June 1949. He claimed that one pilot flew down Tel Aviv's main street at rooftop height, enabling him to approach Sde Dov from the south.

Although the Negev Squadron's airfield at Nir Am was another important REAF target on this first day, most attention was clearly focused upon Sde Dov. Here one of the first bombs is known to have damaged the hangar while another badly damaged an Air France Dakota (F-BAXH). This first pass concluded with a steep turn after which the Egyptian pilot, now known to be *Qa'id Asrab* Abu Zaid, made a strafing run, damaging a number of aeroplanes that were dispersed along the sides of the main runway. A second Spitfire, which had previously been giving cover to his leader, then made a strafing pass before both Spitfires disappeared out to sea. The crews of a number of defending anti-aircraft guns are said to have been asleep at this early hour.

The damage inflicted by the two REAF Spitfires proved to be considerable. An ammunition store had been set on fire, a hanger damaged, Republic RC-3 Seabee VQ-PAV (now of IAF Squadron A, serial 60) and RWD-13 (VQ-PAM) destroyed along with an Air France DC-3, plus several other aircraft damaged. These were a Dragon Rapide (VQ-PAR), two Austers (VQ-PAL/3 and VQ-PAI/5), one irreparably, along with a Bonanza belonging to Boris Senior, the CO at Sde Dov, and a Dakota of Pan African airlines (ZS-AVK). According to a Russian source, a second RWD-13 (VQ-PAL)

Barakat's Spitfire in the process of being salvaged. Notable are the details of the camouflage on the top surfaces of the right wing, and the application of only the green surfaces of the roundel there. (Dr. David Nicolle collection)

Another view of Barakat's aircraft, this time being loaded by crane onto a truck for transport to Sde Dov/Ramat David Air Base. (Dr. David Nicolle collection)

was also damaged, though not apparently seriously, along with two unidentified Tiger Moths. Other sources put the Tel Aviv Squadron's losses as six aeroplanes destroyed or damaged beyond repair. There were several casualties and the Israeli squadron based at Sde Dov was out of action for a while.

It was during a second REAF attack on Sde Dov aerodrome later in the morning that the first Egyptian aeroplane was lost. It was flown by Mahmud Barakat and a great deal of attention has been focused on this machine. Amongst those who watched it being recovered from the beach near Herzliyya was a 10-year-old boy named Amnon Yogev who distinctly remembers its grey and green camouflage, along with its green and white national markings. The latter consisted only of three concentric rings and lacked a white crescent and three small stars on the inner circle. The Spitfire also had no visible serial number. This suggests that it had either been rushed to al-Arish before being fully marked or was one of those which remained unmarked so that they could fly over Palestine before the official Egyptian intervention. This *Qa'id Asrab* Muhammad Abu Zaid did on 14 May. When the author interviewed ex-REAF fighter pilot Tahir Zaki, the old man remembered some Spitfires lacking crescent and stars and added that their serial numbers were only added after the loss of Mahmud Barakat. If Tahir Zaki's memory was correct, he was referring to some rather than to all REAF Spitfires at al-Arish at this time.

Qa'id Sirb Mahmud Barakat had been flying as *Qa'id Asrab* Abu Zaid's wingman. He subsequently described his experiences to a fellow prisoner of war, Abd al-Rahman Inan whom Barakat had obliged to step aside so that Barakat could take part in the first raid. Mahmud Barakat was currently second-in-command of No. 2 Squadron at al-Arish so Inan, as a junior officer, would have had little say in the matter. As Barakat himself stated; 'Our aim was to visit Tel Aviv aerodrome [Sde Dov] for the second time, and this was still in the early hours of the war. Qa'id Asrab Abd al-Hamid Abu Zaid dropped a large bomb on the airfield then flew around for a second bombing run, dropping two smaller bombs.' Meanwhile Barakat flew cover, ready to make his own attack.

The official Egyptian account stated that Barakat's Spitfire was hit by small-arms fire and that he was injured. Barakat's own account stated that he dropped two incendiary bombs, after which both aircraft made a second attack. He felt a shock on the front of his fuselage after which the coolant temperature rose rapidly. However, he jettisoned his remaining bombs on the aerodrome. Eventually the propeller stopped spinning and Barakat 'felt that everything

In a scene from the movie *A Girl from Palestine*, REAF pilots and ground crew at Hilwan re-enacted an emergency scramble for the benefit of the camera. One of the Spitfire LF.Mk 9s (upper right) had its spinner painted in light admiralty grey, while the Spitfire LF.Mk 9 (lower left) had it painted in green-white-green. Of particular interest is the Mk. V (lower right) with the front half of the spinner painted in black: this was the aircraft that received the skull and crossbones motif designed by Muhammad Abu Zaid. (Dr. David Nicolle collection)

was over for him and that he has not yet retaliated for the innocent [Palestinian] Arabs,' and he was obliged to make an emergency landing north of Tel Aviv. When his Spitfire came down on the beach, he felt a violent jolt as the machine slid along the sand before subsiding with its nose in the sea, looking in Barakat's words 'like a thirsty serpent.' His wireless was no longer working, so Barakat waved to Abu Zaid to show that he was alright. The latter waved back, waggled his wings then flew off to al-Arish.

The downing of an Egyptian Spitfire so early in the campaign was naturally used by the Israeli authorities to boost morale at a critical time. In fact, the 'near miraculous' bringing down of a REAF Spitfire by a single small-calibre gun on the ground was almost viewed as a sign of divine approval.

There are several other accounts of Barakat's downing, including in a letter to the American aviation historian Lon Nordeen, written in 1992 by ex-Israeli Air Force officer Marek M. Halberstadt. He maintained that 'The Egyptian pilot did not crash land, but opened his wheels and landed on the beach. His landing was forced by a head wound inflicted by one of the rifle bullets.' Halberstadt also claimed that the Spitfire was hit by rifle fire, not by a machine gun, as the only available Lewis gun had jammed. On the other hand, Israeli historian Jon Kimche stated that when Egyptian Spitfires raided

Another view of two Spitfires in the same movie scene. The aircraft in the rear is an LF.Mk 9, with serial number 651: to the right is the Mk. V serial 620, with the skull-and-crossbones motif. (Dr. David Nicolle collection)

The emergency scramble re-enacted by REAF personnel at Hilwan for the filming of *A Girl from Palestine* also provided a relatively clear view of the Spitfire V with a skull-and-crossbones motif on its spinner as it taxied past the camera. (Dr. David Nicolle collection)

Tel Aviv, 'one was brought down almost undamaged by a lucky machine-gun bullet in the radiator.' The gunner was reportedly stationed on top of Reading Power Station and his burst of fire hit the Spitfire's starboard coolant radiator, which would certainly cause the engine temperature to rise rapidly as Barakat himself recorded. Observers on the ground further suggested that Barakat flew north, perhaps hoping to make an emergency landing in Palestinian Arab territory or the British-held Haifa Enclave. This would have been closer than the Egyptian-held territory in the south. Nevertheless, he came down about 9km from Sde Dov.

There are various accounts of Mahmud Barakat's capture, though his own recollections published in 1971 have been ignored outside Egypt. Speaking through his fellow captive Abd al-Rahman Inan, Barakat explained that; 'He moved away from his aeroplane and hid behind the sand dunes on the beach, watching soldiers pour torrents of bullets at his crashed machine, then found himself surrounded by fifteen heavily armed Jews.' After he surrendered, they took his pistol, wristwatch, a photograph of his family and a small Koran that had never before left his pocket. Barakat's captors then insulted him and beat him up with their fists. 'One over-enthusiastic soldier hit him on the head with the butt of his gun, making him bleed until blood covered his face and clothes.' Barakat's head wound therefore seems to have been suffered during his capture rather than when his Spitfire was hit by groundfire. Eventually a gun was jabbed at his side and he was forced to run while the soldiers threw stones at him.

Israeli versions are inevitably different and according to Halberstadt's letter, Barakat was captured by two young men and a young woman of the Israeli air arm. Barakat recalled being handcuffed and bundled into an Auster aeroplane (actually a Beechcraft Bonanza) which quickly took off and flew to Sde Dov). After the cuffs were removed, Barakat looked around and smiled when he saw the signs of destruction whereupon one of the guards covered Barakat's eyes, after which he was put into a car which drove through Tel Aviv. The driver was in fact Boris Senior, the Israeli CO at Sde Dov who, having seen the damaged Spitfire head north, flew his damaged Bonanza to Shefayim landing strip. Eventually Senior found Barakat in a small brick small factory, which suggests that the Egyptian came down just north of Arsuf.

Mahmud Barakat's account of his interrogation recalled that he climbed many stairs while still blindfolded before sitting down in

An Avro Anson (serial number 182) of the RIrAF seen in Syria during the Palestine War of 1948. Notable is the camera installation in the nose. The serial number on the rear fuselage is 169. (Tom Cooper collection)

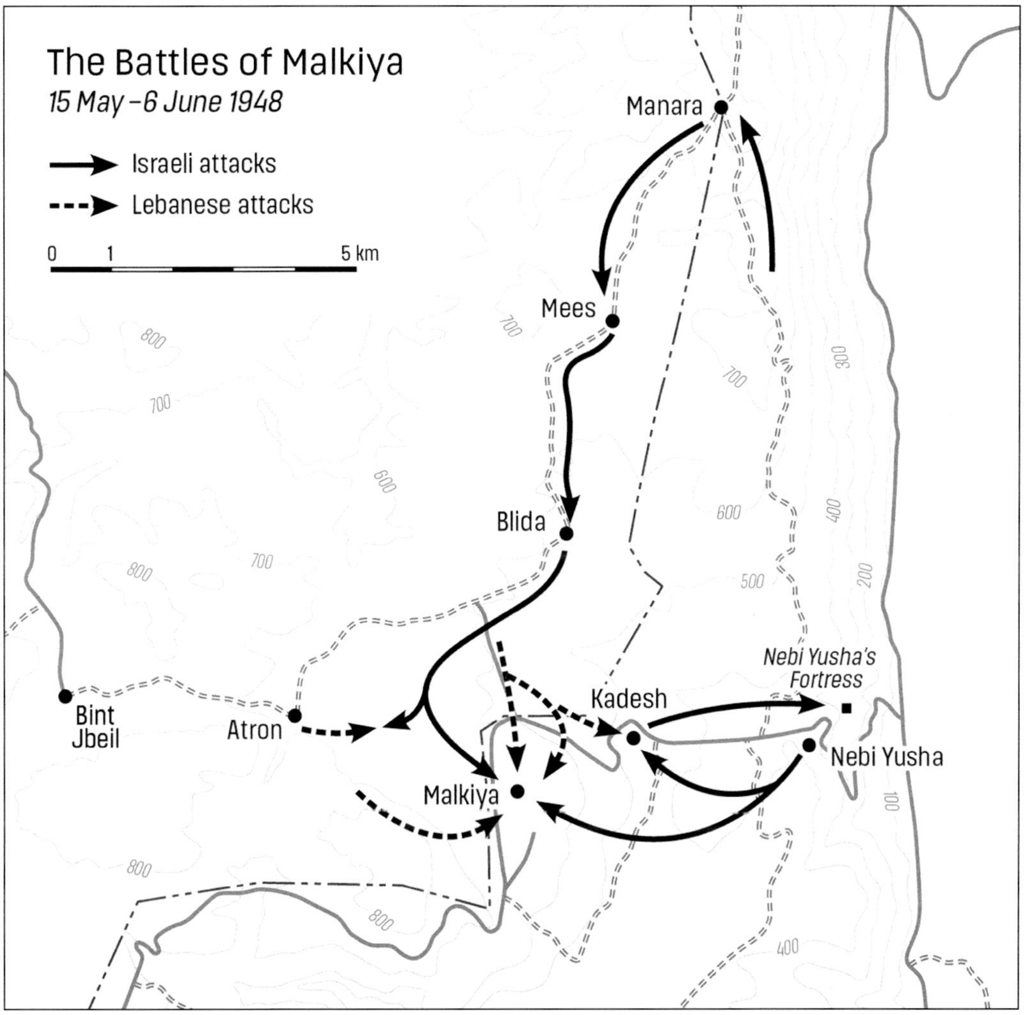

Battles of Malkiya, 15 May – 6 June 1948. (Map by Paul Hewitt)

When interviewed by Jon Kimche, a correspondent for Reuters Press Agency, Mahmud Barakat was reportedly in a one-room bungalow in the garden of the Tel Aviv Regiment's HQ. Unfortunately, Kimche clearly misunderstood some of what Barakat said, thinking that he claimed to be Egypt's second-best pilot after Abd al-Hamid Abu Zaid. In fact, Barakat meant that was second-in-command. In other respects, Kimche's tendentious account claimed that the captured pilot said that; 'We Egyptians have started this war for the British. The British wanted us to liquidate Zionism because it was difficult for them to do so. They told us that we shall not meet any serious opposition.' During this period many supporters of the Zionist project seemed more antagonistic towards the British than they were to the Arabs.

the interrogation room. 'They threatened to use violence when he refused to answer their questions. But he told them that if they did anything, then similar would be meted out to Israeli prisoners in Egyptian hands. Then he was served a fine lunch, this being the first and last time he tasted such good food in Israel.' Barakat was next taken to meet 'the commander of the Tel Aviv area.' Now so thirsty that he felt willing to drink his own blood, Barakat was taken to a room with a bed where he thought about his young son and his infant daughter who was less than a week old.

Another pair of REAF Spitfires made a less successful attack upon Sde Dov around 0800, being met with a barrage of small-arms fire. The final REAF attack on Sde Dov on 15 May came shortly before dusk, just after South African Naftali Blau landed a Fairchild Argus after a long flight from Rome. By the end of the day six aeroplanes of the Tel Aviv Squadron had been destroyed or damaged beyond repair, while others suffered less damage and were later repaired. In the meantime, the Israelis hurriedly dispersed their serviceable and less-damaged aeroplanes, some to Haifa, others to an emergency airstrip near Sharona or to Aqir (Tel Nof) outside Rehovot. One damaged Dakota (ZS-AVK) arrived at Tel Nof shortly after an attack by REAF

Spitfires, a jeep full of armed men roaring up, fearing that Egyptian airborne troops were trying to capture the aerodrome.

REAF sorties against Sde Dov were the most publicised Egyptian air attacks, but there were several others south of Gaza. The first were carried out at the same time as the initial raid on Sde Dov, all reportedly being attacked by pairs of Spitfires. These targets included fortified settlements at Nir Am, Kfar Darom and Negba, some of which had airstrips. Returning Egyptian pilots also claimed several Israeli aircraft damaged on the ground at Nir Am, though this was denied by the Israelis. Around the same time a pair of RAF No. 6 Squadron Tempests encountered a solitary REAF Spitfire strafing a position north of Gaza. As the Egyptian aircraft completed its attack, the British pilots trailed it southwards and then overtook the Egyptian who then himself followed the Tempests before breaking away towards al-Arish.

Unfortunately, the REAF also hit some remaining British troops on 15 May, the British having stated that their only remaining positions were now within the Haifa Enclave. In each case the REAF pilots mistook them and their vehicles for Israelis. As a result, No. 651 AOP Squadron, a British Army Air Corps unit at al-Buraij between Dayr al-Balah and Gaza, was bombed and strafed, perhaps mistakenly associated with the nearby Israeli settlement of Kfar Darom. All four of No. 1910 Flight's Auster AOP.6s were damaged. Elsewhere a solitary REAF Spitfire attacked a column of British soldiers with anti-personnel bombs at around 0700 in the morning, one soldier of the 2/Kings Royal Rifle Corps being killed and eight others wounded. This was the incident mentioned in No. 6 Squadron RAF's Operations Records Book which stated that; 'This took place at about 1215 consequently all further sorties were briefed to look out for trouble in that area.'

When the British protested, the Egyptian authorities passed on the REAF's apologies but pointed out that the Egyptian Ministry of Defence had not been informed of the presence or the locations of these remaining British forces. Elsewhere the REAF knew that it was attacking ex-RAF bases but had been assured that these had been vacated by the British. One was an aerodrome near Beersheba where unspecified Egyptian aeroplanes claimed to have damaged several buildings and some apparently abandoned, or perhaps Israeli, aircraft.

Information about the activities of other Arab air forces remains very sparce. According to some sources, Iraqi Ansons bombed Israeli forces in or close to the town of Tiberias, whereas other sources deny that the RIrAF flew any offensive missions on Saturday 15 May and that the Iraqi Army's crossing of the river Jordan lacked air cover. Arab Legion units which also crossed the Jordan on the 15th similarly lacked air cover, the REAF not yet offering such support to Transjordanian forces.

In contrast, the Harvards of the tiny SyAAF promptly initiated combat by attacking the fortified Massada and Shaar Hagolan settlements south of Samakh. Information from the Israeli side is more detailed, stating that Syrian aircraft strafed and bombed the two settlements named Degania, as well as the villages of Kinneret, Yavn'eel, and Ein Gev.

During the following night (15–16 May), Peretz Grosser and Avraham Balatyta in an Auster of the Israeli Air Force's Galilee Squadron attempted to bomb the new bridge thrown across the Jordan by Iraqi Army engineers. They failed to hit the target but reportedly set fire to a facility belonging to the Iraq Petroleum Company, probably a pumping station. This reportedly burned for five days but was probably not why a nearby Arab Legion armoured unit moved to a different location.

To the northwest, surviving aircraft from Israel's Tel Aviv Squadron helped Israeli forces push back Lebanese troops who had occupied a police fortress next to the village of al-Nabi Yusha', south of al-Malkiyah. Shortly after dawn, the Lebanese force under Brigadier General Fu'ad Shihab mounted a successful counterattack, forcing the Israelis back from Qadas and al-Malkiyah with 120 dead and wounded. After occupying al-Malkiyah, a significant Lebanese force advanced towards Qadas from which the *Palmach* battalion withdrew, allowing from the village to be taken by Lebanese troops.

16 MAY 1948

Ground Operations

After seizing al-Malkiyah and Qadas, Brigadier Shihab decided to halt the Lebanese advance and consolidate his position before resuming an advance. In contrast, during the afternoon of 16 May the Iraqis launched their main attack upon Gesher and the neighbouring police fortress, but due to a lack of coordination this attack failed. At 1930 hrs the following evening, an Egyptian report based upon the Iraqi Army HQ report presented this setback in the best light possible, stating that; 'Iraqi artillery and aircraft poured down shells and bombs on the Gesher colony, which was severely damaged. The Iraqi Air Force also bombed Baysan very effectively.' Israeli sources merely stated that RlrAF Ansons bombed Tiberias and Beit Yosef in the Jordan Valley but caused little damage.

To the south, a *Palmach* force was reported to have broken into the Old City of Jerusalem through the Zion Gate during the evening of 16 May, making contact with the defenders of the Jewish Quarter. In fact, a major battle had developed in Jerusalem and King Abdullah now realised that there was no real hope of establishing a permanent truce here. In fact, General Glubb came under strong pressure from Abdullah to save Jerusalem, the monarch's insistence stemming from the importance of Jerusalem as Islam's third Holy City, the loss of which to the Israelis would have a disastrous effect upon Transjordan's – and indeed his own – reputation across the Muslim world. Nevertheless, General Glubb still hesitated and sent only the 1st and 8th Companies of the 6th Battalion to occupy the Mount of Olives, overlooking the eastern side of the Old City.

On what became the Syrian front, Israeli settlements were subjected to artillery bombardment and air attacks, followed by ground assaults during the morning of 16 May. The Syrian force that targeted Samakh succeeded in containing an Israeli reserve unit approaching from Tiberias and also occupied a military camp south of the village. Seen from the Israeli side, this resulted in a desperate battle in which the Syrian advance was halted, but at the cost of all but one member of the Israeli troops defending the village. Elsewhere the Israeli defenders of Massada and Shaar Hagolan also held off a Syrian attack.

Elsewhere Israeli units had moved quickly on the termination of the British Mandate to occupy territory beyond the boundaries of the Jewish state specified by the Partition Resolution. Some operations which started just before the termination of the Mandate also continued, including Operation *Qilshon* (Pitchfork) which seized additional areas in and around Jerusalem immediately they were evacuated by the British.

A number of Palestinian villages had similarly been captured in the south and Israeli settlements in the Negev, which had been almost isolated since the coastal road was blocked by irregular Arab forces at the end of March 1948, could now be reached by a new track running roughly parallel to the ancient coastal road. In the meantime, a new Zionist settlement was established at Bror Hayil to neutralise any threat to the new track from the Palestinian village of Burair which itself soon fell to an Israeli force. The latter then headed north to capture al-Hulaiqat and Kawkaba which also fell with minimal resistance. Thus Israeli communications with the Negev were now opened – for a while.

Air Operations

According to a Syrian GHQ communique broadcast at 2000 hrs GMT on 16 May the SyAAF 'successfully bombed Rosh Pina airfield.... The town of Tiberias was also bombed.' Israeli sources stated that six Harvard sorties targeted the area of Tiberias, Afikim and Ashdot Ya'akov, the SyAAF using three pairs of aircraft which dropped a total of 12 bombs, two hitting their targets.

Egyptian troops having tea by the roadside during the Palestine War. It has been suggested that the man in the centre was an Israeli negotiator during a pause in the fighting. (Dr. David Nicolle collection)

There was meanwhile a rare mention of Saudi Arabian transport aeroplanes, Cairo Radio reporting at 1930 on 17th May that;

> A spokesman of the Kingdom of Saudi Arabia told the Arab News Agency that the Army of Saudi Arabia had taken part in the fighting since the night of 16th May, in cooperation with the Egyptian Army. Saudi Arabian aircraft have been transporting troops since the morning of the 16th to the Egyptian front; Egyptian and Saudi Arabian ships are transporting troops and supplies, and in a few days the Saudi Arabian troops will take part in the fighting beside the Transjordanian and Iraqi forces.

At this time Saudi Arabia had some civilian passenger aircraft under the authority of the Saudi Ministry of Defence, but it seems likely that some of the transports involved in this airlift were Egyptian.

17 MAY 1948

On 17 May, the United States submitted a draft resolution which declared that the situation in Palestine was a threat to peace under the UN Charter, requesting a ceasefire within 36 hours and threatening sanctions against any party failing to comply. However, on British insistence this draft was amended, deleting mention of the UN Charter, before it was passed on 22 May. Meanwhile, the Arab states defended their action, arguing that the existing Partition Resolution became void when the UN General Assembly dissolved the Palestine Commission. They also maintained that, with the termination of the British Mandate, Palestine became an independent nation where the Zionist Jews constituted a rebellious minority. Israel was not, they maintained, legally a state.

Ground Operations

On 17 May, Colonel Abd al-Rahman Aziz and the Egyptian Light Force pressed forward towards Beersheba. The main Egyptian Army thrust headed for al-Majdal which was almost reached by the end of the day, though some heavily defended and fortified Israeli settlements were bypassed and blockaded on the way. Fighting had been fierce on this Egyptian front, but Israeli forces were obliged to retreat. The strategically placed ex-British police fort outside Iraq Suwaidan was apparently handed over by Muslim Brotherhood volunteers to another Muslim Brotherhood unit under Egyptian command on 17th or 18 May.

Meanwhile Iraqi forces renewed their assault upon Gesher during the morning of 17 May, with infantry advancing from the north and armoured cars from the south, but this attack was again repulsed. Encouraged by this Iraqi failure, the Israelis attempted to capture the nearby Camel stronghold but they in turn failed. As a result, Gesher was surrounded. Elsewhere, Israeli troops continued to seize Palestinian Arab territory, including the village of Qatra 15kms southwest of Ramlah; its population being expelled. The Israeli high command had also decided to launch their planned assault upon the Old City of Jerusalem on the evening of the 17th but due to administrative problems this was delayed for 24 hours.

At 2330 hrs on 17 May, King Abdullah, who was furious at General Glubb's slowness, took two important steps, going over Glubb's head and ordered Major Abdullah al-Tal – the commander of the 6th Regiment – to save the Old City while urging Glubb to advance towards Jerusalem to force its Jewish defenders to accept a truce. Glubb had meanwhile discovered that ALA irregulars in Latrun had abandoned their positions without notifying the Arab Legion, having expected the latter to replace them on 15 May. Thus Glubb had to move against Israeli forces in Jerusalem while also blocking the road from Tel Aviv, to stop the stream of Israeli reinforcements which had been arriving in Jerusalem over the previous two days. The 4th Regiment was therefore pulled out of Ramallah to occupy the abandoned Latrun positions while the 1st Company on the Mount of Olives was sent to reinforce Arab defenders in the Old City.

On the Syrian front, the second day of Arab intervention saw the Syrians repeat their attack on Samakh, following an artillery bombardment. Israeli reinforcements which hurried from neighbouring settlements helped the defenders hold on until the morning of 18th May when their positions collapsed, Syrian troops then occupying the village.

Air Operations

On 17 May, as the Egyptian Army's advance continued, the REAF continued its attacks upon Sde Dov airfield. During the morning Tel Aviv harbour was also attacked, with Egyptian Spitfire pilots claiming that their bombs hit quays, oil tanks and refineries. The Israelis reported that three civilians were killed. REAF Spitfires returned to Tel Aviv and Sde Dov during the afternoon, claiming to have damaged six small aeroplanes and some airfield facilities. The Israeli side admitted that two Austers (numbers A-1 and A-31) were damaged.

There were also raids against the ex-RAF aerodrome at Kfar Sirkin airfield and Negba, Egyptian reports claiming that Kfar Sirkin was rendered unserviceable and that all REAF aeroplanes returned safely. This broadcast was followed at 2200 hrs GMT by another quoting the Egyptian Ministry of Defence's Communique No. 5 summarising Egyptian actions on 17 May;

> Military operations began with wide reconnaissance operations on all fronts.... Early in the morning, our bombers dropped high explosives and incendiaries on the fortifications of the settlement of Shdimuth, registering hits on fuel and ammunition stores and on groups of armoured cars inside the settlement. When the planes left, fires were raging everywhere inside the settlement. A squadron of the REAF attacked the port of Tel Aviv this morning, registering direct hits on the quays, petrol tanks, and oil installations, setting them on fire. The Air Force attacked the airfield of Tel Aviv (Sde Dov) this afternoon, destroying six planes on the airfield and causing considerable damage. Reports and photographs show that all these raids were successful and all our planes returned successfully to their bases.

This Egyptian broadcast appears to contain the first reference to a target called Shdimuth, as hurriedly written down by the BBC's Monitoring Service at Caversham Park west of London, or as Shidimu when in the REAF Tactical Air Force Operational Diary. Israeli historian Meiri Ilan has suggested there were two possible locations, Moshav Shdema about 1km east of the main road between Isdud and Yibna, about 4.5km south of Yibna, but there seems no obvious reason why the REAF should attack this small location. However, the headquarter of the Negev Brigade was for a while Shdemot, less than a kilometre west of Nir Am and its airfield. This was certainly attacked on a number of occasions and is most likely to be the REAF target called Shidimu or Shdimuth. Meanwhile, Israeli reports concerning REAF attacks on 17 May are somewhat dismissive, a *Haganah* communique broadcast at 1800 hrs claiming that; 'Enemy aircraft flew over Tel Aviv, dropped bombs indiscriminately, but were driven off by a heavy barrage put up by the Jewish defenders.'

The BBC Monitoring Service also transcribed an Iraqi news report, broadcast from Baghdad at 2000 hrs GMT the following day, stating that: 'Iraqi aircraft raided and bombed all Jewish colonies yesterday [17 May], causing heavy damage.' Obviously not all Israel settlements had been attacked, so the claim presumably referred to those currently under pressure from the Iraqi Army. More specific information about RIrAF sorties came in a broadcast from Cairo at 2200 hrs GMT on 17 May; 'The Iraqi High Command issued a communique in Baghdad tonight stating that the Royal Iraqi Air Force raided the Zionist settlements of Gesher, Yousef [unidentified],

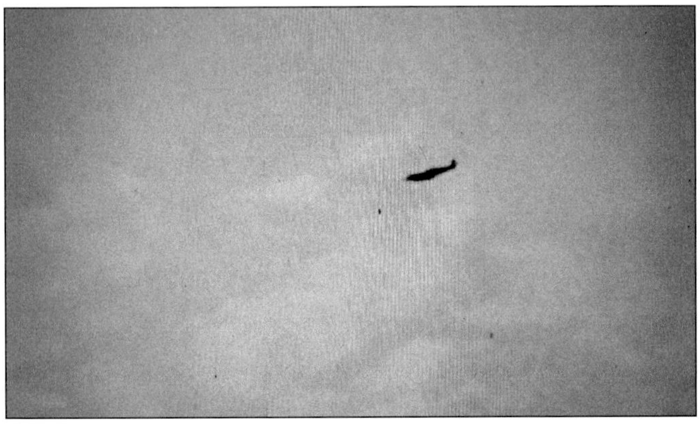

A Spitfire of the REAF seen in a dive on a target in the Tel Aviv area in May 1948. (Dr. David Nicolle collection)

A Spitfire LF.Mk 9 of the REAF seen turning at low altitude over Tel Aviv in May 1948. Notable are the 20mm guns, and roundels applied unusually close to the wingtips. (Dr. David Nicolle collection)

and Majdal [one of several locations with this name in Palestine]. Fires were seen to take hold of these settlements.'

The clearest picture of SyAAF operations over northern Palestine is gained by combining several sources. At 1930 hrs GMT a Cairo broadcast stated that; 'Arab aircraft raided Tiberias and inflicted heavy damage on the Jewish airfield of Rosh Pinna.' These were presumably Syrian aircraft as a Syrian official communique from Damascus at 2050 GMT stated that; 'Our aircraft brought down an enemy plane on Lake Tiberias. The Syrian Air Force attacked.... a colony west of Banat Yaqoub [Jisr Banat Ya'qub]. Direct hits were scored and fires broke out which could be seen ten miles away. Our planes bombed Tiberias and sank two enemy ships.' The latter were small patrol boats.

Israeli sources reported that two Syrian Harvards chased an Israeli Auster flown by Menachem Bernstein of the Galilee Squadron during an incident described in detail by a member of kibbutz Ein Gev who recalling that;

> At about 1700 one of our Primuses [the nickname given to Auster light aircraft] appeared above the Syrian village of Harb. When it crossed the border and flew inside Syrian territory, a couple of Spitfires [actually Harvards] were scrambled and the noise of machine guns was heard. Then, the Primus flew south trying to escape them but they caught up with it and tried to leap on it. This brought our comrades out of their trenches and we anxiously watched the uneven dogfight. When the aircraft reached Zemah [Samakh], the Primus suddenly lost height and we were certain it was hit.

The Harvards continued to dive on the unseen Auster until they finally climbed away. The member of kibbutz Ein Gev continued; 'After a few seconds of tension and frustration we saw the Primus flying slowly over the Yavn'eel hills.' The Syrian pilots were nevertheless sure that they had destroyed the Auster. Moreover, during the chase they found the Galilee Squadron's Yavn'eel airstrip which the SyAAF had been seeking since the start of the conflict, resulting in it no longer being safe for Israeli operations. The Israelis also recorded that a single Harvard attacked the Nabi al-Yusha' police fort on the 17th.

Within the British-occupied Haifa Enclave it was decided that on 17th and 18 May the Tempest detachment of No. 249 Squadron and the Lancasters of Nos. 37 and 38 Squadrons should at last depart. Ramat David aerodrome would be vacated by 24 May with the two Spitfire squadrons moving out on the 22nd. The scene was thus set for a tragedy.

A 6-pdr anti-tank gun of the Egyptian Army mounted on the back of a lorry, reportedly in action during the siege of Yad Mordechai. (Dr. David Nicolle collection)

18 MAY 1948

Ground Operations

Both sides agree that the Battle of Yad Mordechai was a major event during the Palestine War. On 18 May, General al-Muwawi had intended to resume his advance towards al-Majdal, the Egyptian Army's next major objective after taking Gaza. This time, however, he decided that the Israeli settlement of Yad Mordechai was too dangerous to be left behind as it would dominate the line of advance. This extensive, strongly fortified location also served as the main supply centre for Israeli settlements in the Negev and must therefore be taken. So al-Muwawi committed one of his three infantry battalions to its conquest, Yad Mordechai eventually falling on 24 May after very hard fighting.

Elsewhere on the southern front, Israeli forces launched their first serious attempt to take Iraq Suwaidan, the main Israel attack being made from the south-west. It failed but around the same time the large Arab village of al-Maghar, plus the smaller Sawafir al-Shamaliya, Sawafir al-Gharbiya and Sawafir al-Sharqiya fell to the Givati Brigade. Most of the inhabitants of al-Maghar ended up in the Maghazi Refugee Camp in the Gaza Strip, along with people from Yazur, Qastina, Batani al-Sharqi, Batani al-Gharbi and other obliterated villages. Meanwhile additional Muslim Brotherhood units landed by ship at al-Majdal and proceeded to reinforce Egyptian positions along the lateral road linking Iraq Suwaidan and Bayt Jibrin.

The arrival of a Jordanian company at the walls of Jerusalem raised the morale of its Palestinian defenders and when the Etzioni troops mounted their main assault during the evening the Arab defenders were waiting for them. The attackers were defeated with heavy loss, their armoured cars were dispersed and the Israeli troops spent the rest of the night evacuating their dead and wounded. Unlike the Etzioni units, the Harel Brigade was successful, capturing Mount Zion then blowing a breach in the Zion Gate to link up with the defenders of the Jewish Quarter. Next morning, however, Major al-Tal's Legionnaires counterattacked, expelling most of the Harel troops and blocking the Zion Gate once more. Nevertheless, around 80 Harel men with substantial quantities of ammunition remained to bolster the defenders of the Jewish Quarter.

A REAF reconnaissance photograph of Yad Mordechai. (Dr. David Nicolle collection)

A trio of REAF C-47 Skytrain/Dakotas in flight during the Palestine War. Records indicate that no more than three were used together on a bombing raid. (Dr. David Nicolle collection)

On the Syrian front, Israeli positions in Samakh collapsed during the morning, under pressure from Syrian troops who then occupied the village. Meanwhile, *Haganah* command sent *Palmach* reinforcements to the nearby twin settlements of Degania Alef and Degania Bet which became the Israeli front line.

Air Operations

On the afternoon of 18 May, anti-aircraft guns in Cairo opened fire. Whether this was an exercise or someone thought they saw an enemy aeroplane remains unknown although it might have been part of a campaign to encourage volunteer to join the Egyptian armed forces. There clearly were significant efforts in this direction and the following day Radio Cairo announced that 'many pilots wanted to volunteer for service.'

As was normal at this stage of the Arab-Israeli conflict, the Israelis were prone to blame the British rather than blaming the Arab states. Thus, on three successive days after the downing of Barakat's Spitfire, Israeli Radio's daily Arabic news bulletin claimed that Egyptian aeroplanes had been 'painted over recently to hide the British markings.' On the 18th it was announced that the pilot of a downed Egyptian plane was found to be 'carrying instructions in English' – English still being widely used in the REAF – while on the 19th a bulletin stated that that 'the paint used to put on the Egyptian markings on the plane which we brought down was still wet and the British markings could be seen underneath.' This, it was claimed, identified the true 'political murderer who crosses our frontier, attacks our villages and cities, spreading death and destruction everywhere. This is a British attack disguised as an Arab one.'

Tuesday 18 May also saw the REAF's first recorded use of two C-47 'Dakota bombers' which, accompanied by two Spitfires, struck strategic targets in Tel Aviv. The central transport depot was damaged and a fuel dump was claimed destroyed, resulting in 42 casualties, including civilians. Other evidence suggests that there were two raids; the fuel depot being attacked by Spitfires early in the morning while the Dakota raid on the bus station took place in the afternoon. One of these Dakota bombers was piloted by Abd al-Latif Baghdadi with Wagih Abaza as co-pilot, indicating that Abaza had duties other than pilfering from British military depots along the Suez Canal. According to Baghdadi's account of his role during the conflict, he sometimes flew five or six times a day, and attacked the Tel Aviv area several times, including a night raid or raids later in the war.

This first 'Dakota bomber' raid was witnessed by a REAF Spitfire pilot who had been shot down earlier in the day while attacking the Israeli fuel depot. Like Mahmud Barakat, 22-year-old *Tayyar Awal* Gamal Irfan Sayf al-Nasr from Upper Egypt later told his story to Abd al-Rahman Inan when all three were held as prisoners-of-war. Six aircraft had taken off at 0500 on the morning, led by *Qa'id Asrab* Muhammad Abd al-Hamid Abu Zaid. As Gamal Irfan explained;

> The aeroplanes start to dive one after another and from my position in the rear aircraft I saw air defence fire at every aircraft that came to shoot at the [fuel] tanks. I also saw bombs hit the stores and make a big explosion and a big fire. When it was my turn to drop my incendiary bombs, I realised that there was no need to drop them because all the tanks were already on fire, but I dropped anyway. Then the aircraft returned to hit the target with their guns. I was at the back to protect the [other] aircraft and when I went down to strafe the target with guns, I felt shock in my engine and white smoke began to appear. So, I gained altitude and headed towards the Arab region in the south, praying to God that I would reach this Arab region safely. For a while I felt that God was helping me but I could see that the smoke was increasing a great deal and soon I was suffocating from the smoke. Then the engine stopped completely and there was no alternative except to make an emergency landing close to Tel Aviv.

Irfan came down close to extensive orange groves near Rishon-le-Zion, glanced off a cement wall, struck his head hard on the bombsight, was for a while unconscious then hurried out of his smoking aeroplane. The official Egyptian Communique No. 6, broadcast from Cairo at 2200 on the 18th, claimed a major success but also admitted the loss of Irfan's Spitfire, while the Israeli military command again sought to involve the British by noting that Irfan's Spitfire 'bore British markings which had been freshly painted over.'

Like Mahmud Barakat before him, Gamal Irfan Sayf al-Nasr had little chance of escaping capture, although he tried walking east, towards the hills of what is now the West Bank, behind which the sun was rising. At this stage of the conflict Gamal Irfan would only have had to walk between three and five kilometres to reach territory still controlled by Palestinian Arab militias. Despite a strong pain in his chest, he kept going for about 45 minutes, then, perhaps nearing the front-line, he found himself facing five Israeli soldiers with Sten guns;

> I understood from their leader that I needed to raise my hands, but they remained in their position without moving, shouting at me in apparent terror. They seemed afraid of me because the flying helmet which I had taken off my head was still in my hand. So, I threw it to the ground, which reassured them and their faces relaxed.

Irfan was then taken to a ruined building, probably part of the demolished Palestinian Arab village of Sarafand al-Kharab. After a while his captors took him to the small Israeli town of Ness Ziona. It

Originally assigned to the Royal Air Force's No. 651 Squadron, which was disbanded at the end of 1947, this Taylorcraft Auster AOP.6 – serial VF502 – was left behind at Ramat David until the British withdrawal. Thereafter it was re-assigned to No. 1909 Flight, RAF, based in the Haifa enclave. When the latter was evacuated, it was flown – perhaps with two other Austers of the same unit – to Amman, placed at the disposal of the UN (without crews) and painted in white overall, with the black title UNITED NATIONS on the fuselage side. It is possible that the title was not repeated on the wings before the machine was badly damaged on the ground on 25 June 1948 by a pair of REAF Spitfires whose pilots thought it was an Israeli aircraft because its overall white livery looked similar to the overall silver dope on Israeli-operated Austers. Several of No. 651 Squadron's other Austers had in fact been sold to Aviron which served as a front organisation for *Sherut Avir* which in turn became the Israeli Air Force. This aircraft was eventually returned to the RAF but was promptly struck off charge on 10 February 1949. (Artwork by Tom Cooper)

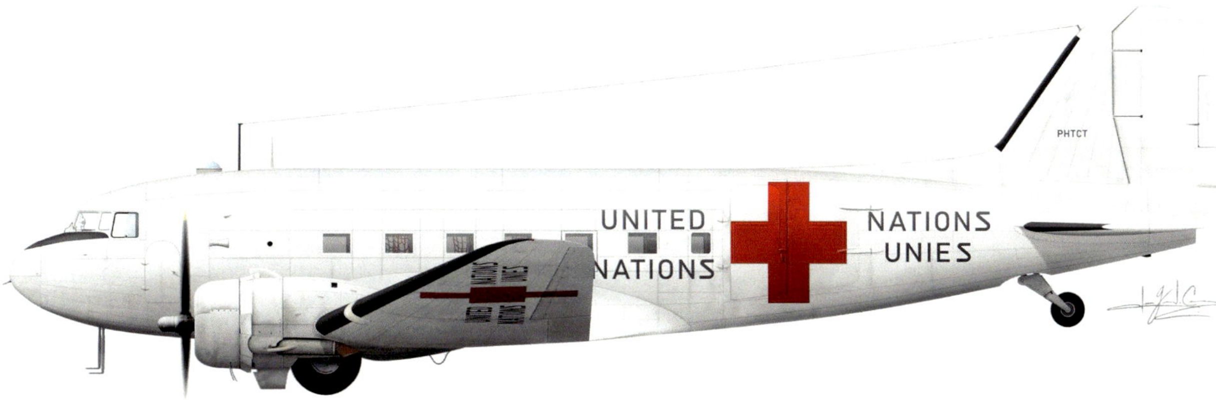

This Douglas C-47 Skytrain operated by the United Nations was provided to Folke Bernadotte, Count of Wisborg (1895–1948), while he was serving as the United Nations Mediator in Palestine. Bernadotte had become famous for organising exchanges of over 11,000 prisoners from Germany during the Second World War, and for rescuing 15,000 people from German concentration camps. On 20 May 1948, he was tasked by the United Nations with negotiating a truce between unilaterally declared Israel and its Arab enemies. However, Count Bernadotte would be assassinated by the Jewish terrorist group *Lehi*, commonly known in the West as the Stern Gang, on 17 September 1948. (Artwork by Luca Canossa)

A handful of reconditioned Gloster Gladiator Mk. IIs of No. 4 Squadron Royal Iraqi Air Force were deployed to Mafraq shortly before the Palestine War. These aircraft retained their high-speed silver overall finish (except for the darkened bronze finish on the front of the engine cowling), and propellers remained black with yellow tips. They wore national markings in six standard positions plus a large serial number on the rear fuselage, in this instance 202. The black inscription on the fuselage below the cockpit hood is not entirely clear in the only available photograph, but appears to have been *Jass 4* in Arabic, meaning 'Reconnaissance 4'. The deployment of Iraqi Gladiators to Jordan was marred by the poor technical condition of these old and virtually worn-out machines. One is known to have crashed while en route to Amman, after which the remainder flew top-cover for Iraqi Ansons. Nevertheless, the words Jass 4 might suggest that they had originally been intended for front-line reconnaissance work. (Artwork by Peter Penev)

Generally, Avro Anson Mk Is deployed by the Royal Iraqi Air Force to Jordan and Syria during the Arab-Israeli War of 1948 were painted in silver dope overall. National insignia still covered the entire rudder and sloped down the line of the rudder hinge. Many had their dorsal gunner's turret removed, and a clear astrodome immediately behind the cockpit still in place, as shown here. Unlike the Egyptian examples, their engine cowlings were smooth. National markings were applied in six positions, while many had their serial numbers – 181 in this case – reapplied in much larger Arabic script than on other Iraqi examples. (Artwork by Tom Cooper)

Another RIrAF Anson known to have been deployed to Mafraq in Jordan – and probably to Damascus in Syria – was serial number 182: one of the rare examples for which there are several photographs available. Originally, this aircraft had its serial number applied on the rear fuselage, and then repeated – in much smaller digits – on the nose. By 1948, and unusually, (though as in the case of the 181) the serial number was reapplied in Arabic script on the rear fuselage only, with the central digit ٨ slightly lower than ١ and ٢. More importantly, by 1948, this aircraft lost its dorsal machine gun turret. (Artwork by Tom Cooper)

Numerous Anson Mk 1s drawn from Nos. 1 and 7 Squadrons Royal Iraqi Air Force for deployment to Jordan and Syria in 1948 retained their dorsal turret with machine gun, but had no astrodome above the cockpit. Moreover, as of May and June 1948, they had their noses painted green – apparently in the same shade as that used for their national markings. This example was photographed while wearing this livery and its serial number on the rear fuselage – 189 in this case – still applied in the original format: with digits in Arabic script at the top, and Arab numerals below. Iraqi Ansons were primarily deployed as light bombers, but severe shortages of spares, bombs, and ammunition greatly hampered their operations. (Artwork by Tom Cooper)

Douglas C-47 Dakota/Skytrain transports continued providing faithful service to the REAF throughout the Palestine War. Such aircraft retained their bare metal overall finish with a black anti-glare panel in front of the cockpit. Notable on this example – serial number 810 – the rear undersides of the engine nacelles are painted in black, as were rotor heads, and the serial repeated underneath the wing. Rather unusual was the form in which the underwing roundels were applied: these had a rather narrow central ring in white. This aircraft appears to have never been forward-deployed at el-Arish for any longer period of time, because it is not mentioned in the parts of the Tactical Air Force Operation Diary that are available. (Artwork by Luca Canossa)

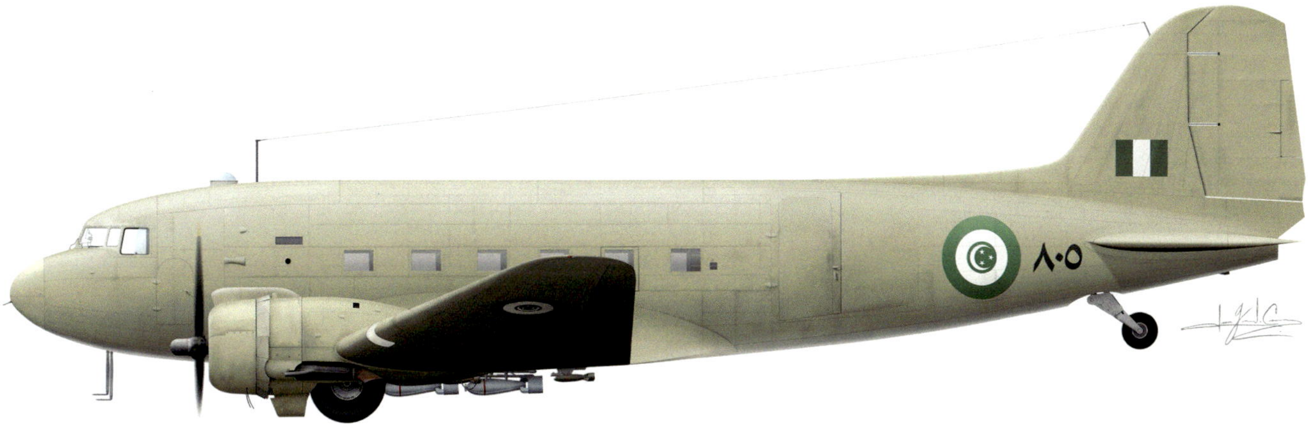

In contrast, this C-47 Dakota/Skytrain 'bomber' of the REAF – serial number 805 – is shown as it appeared while operated by the Tactical Air Force at el-Arish in the early days of the Palestine War. It was painted in overall light sand colour, probably worn by all REAF 'bombers' early during the conflict. However, after appearing in an early Egyptian news reel, it was never mentioned in the available pages of the Tactical Air Force Operation Diary, or in the available logbooks: possibly, this was the aircraft damaged by an Israeli fighter and forced to make an emergency landing on 3 June 1948 (when the Israeli pilot was falsely credited with 'destruction of two Egyptian bombers'). The aircraft wore national markings in the usual six positions, and fin flashes, while the serial 805 was applied in black on the rear fuselage, but not repeated under the wings. (Artwork by Luca Canossa)

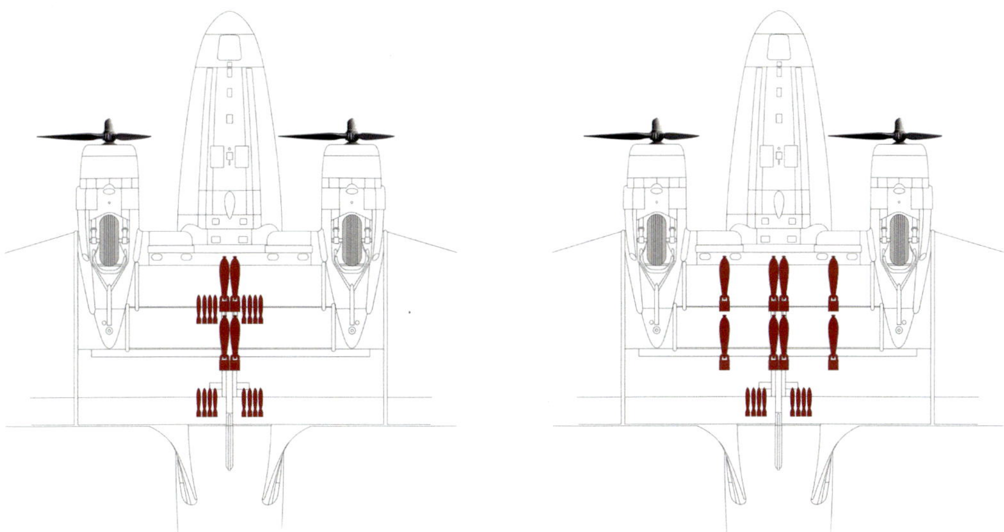

These diagrams show the two known patterns in which external bomb racks were attached under the fuselages and inboard wing sections of the REAF's C-47 'bombers.' Reportedly, all the racks were taken from redundant Avro Ansons, though the sheer number of available Dakota 'bombers' known suggests that other sources were also available, perhaps including British and US dumps left in Egypt after the Second World War. The main racks for the four larger bombs were attached to the fuselage close to the mid-wing point and either side of this point where the wings met the fuselage. Additional racks were attached further back, close to where the trailing edges of the wings flared into the fuselage. (Diagram by Luca Canossa)

All Supermarine Spitfire F/LF.Mk 9s operated by the REAF were painted in BS381C/638 Dark Sea Grey and BS381C/641 Dark Green on their upper surfaces, with BS381C/697 Light Admiralty Grey on their undersurfaces. Over 40 were acquired by Cairo but their exact number operated by REAF remains unknown: the only thing certain is that they received serials in the range from 621 to 679 (not necessarily assigned sequentially). All Egypt's Spitfire Mk 9s were operated by Nos. 1 and 2 Fighter Squadrons. This example, serial number 651, is known to have been one of the most heavily used of its type during the Palestine War and had the front of its spinner painted the same green as used in Egyptian national markings. It was certainly equipped with universal bomb racks under the wings and, according to the Operational Diary of the al-Arish base, it flew at least 25 and perhaps up to 27 or more combat sorties over Palestine between 9 June 1948 and 2 January 1949. (Artwork by Tom Cooper)

REAF Spitfire LF. Mk 9 number 654 wore an alternative version of the standardised camouflage pattern of BS381C/638 Dark Sea Grey and BS381C/641 Dark Green upper surfaces, and BS381C/697 Light Admiralty Grey undersurfaces, with a slightly larger serial number applied on the rear fuselage. Unlike number 651 shown above, this aircraft had two green bands on the front of its spinner. Number 654 is known to have flown three combat sorties over Palestine, on 8 June, and 9 and 15 July 1948. Thereafter, it was probably redeployed to Helwan where it was used for operational training as well as the air defence of Cairo. (Artwork by Tom Cooper)

The skull-and-crossbones motif painted on the spinner of this REAF Spitfire Mk Vc was designed by Squadron Leader Muahmmad Abu Zaid, the CO of Egyptian fighters at al-Arish early during the Palestine War. It was painted on just one side of the spinner. Abu Zaid almost certainly flew this aircraft, but it was also used by other pilots. During the early summer 1948, when the REAF withdrew its old Spitfire Vs to Hilwan, the machine featured in the filming of *A Girl from Palestine*, before being rushed back to the front as the fighting flared up again. The Spitfire Mk Vc with serial number 620 was written off during a combat sortie over Palestine on 18 July 1948, while flown by Squadron Leader al-Janzuri. The pilot died after the crash, indicating that he attempted an emergency landing. (Artwork by Tom Cooper)

On 7 July 1948, when King Farouq visited the REAF base in el-Arish, he was shown at least one of REAF Spitfire F/LF.Mk 9s equipped with a reconnaissance camera. The aircraft's camouflage pattern in Dark Sea Grey and Dark Green on upper surfaces was in a better condition than that of other Spitfires equipped in similar fashion (see next profile), and it had most of national markings applied, but the white fuselage band was removed and its undersurfaces were painted either in BS381C/108 Aircraft Blue, or an even darker colour. Although not shown here, the serial 642 seems to have been applied only about a month later (by when it received universal bomb carriers under the wings), probably for the benefit of news photographers and film crews. Moreover, this aircraft received a score-board for all the aircraft, ground vehicles and other targets claimed by the Tactical Air Force applied on the left side of the fuselage, in front of the cockpit. (Artwork by Tom Cooper)

When forced to land on the beach of Hertzlya following attack on Sde Dov on 15 May 1948, the Spitfire F/LF.Mk 9 piloted by Mahmud Barakat became one of the best known REAF aircraft of the Palestine War. Assembled from parts drawn from several different Seafires and Spitfires abandoned by the British and Americans at different air bases in Egypt towards the end of the Second World War, this was one of the REAF's 'anonymised' Spitfires and lacked any serial number. It received an unusual camouflage pattern in BS381C/638 Dark Sea Grey and BS381C/641 Dark Green on upper surfaces, but an unknown shade of light grey or light blue on undersurfaces. By 15 May 1948, its national markings – deleted for clandestine reconnaissance operations over Palestine flown earlier – were only partially reapplied, and then on the rear fuselage only: those on top wing surfaces lacked the white colour. (Artwork by Peter Penev)

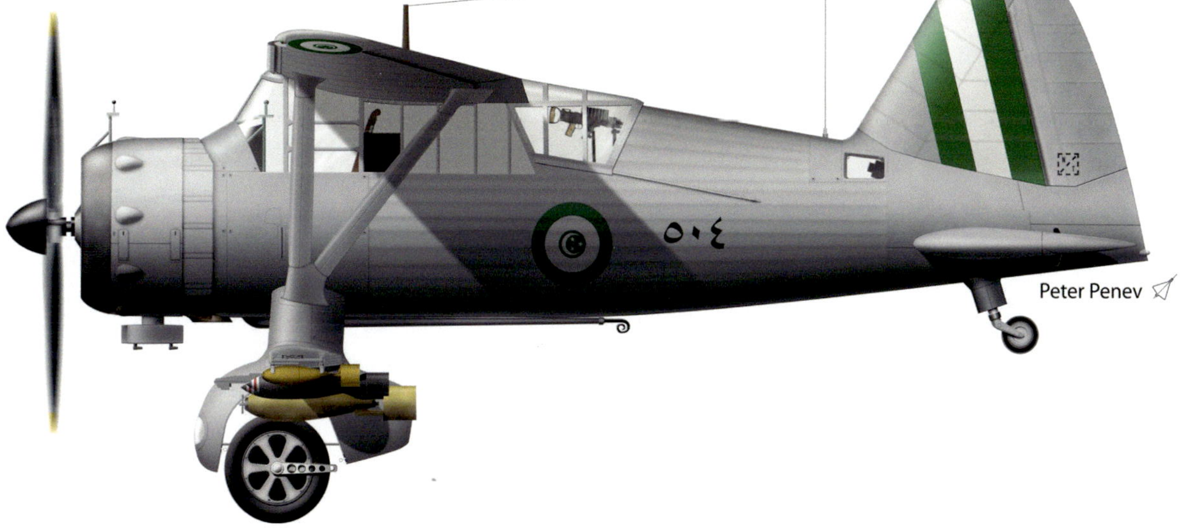

When put through an overhaul in the final years of the Second World War, this Westland Lysander from No. 3 Squadron, REAF – serial number 504 (ex. Y504) – was thoroughly renewed, including the replacement of most fabric, and repainted in overall silver dope. The only significant difference was that the serial number lost the prefix Y, and that this was not reapplied on any other parts of the airframe or the wing. As with all other Lysanders deployed with the Tactical Air Force at al-Arish, it had the side panels of the wheel spats removed, and the short version of stub wings with bomb racks installed instead. Lysander serial number 504 is known to have flown at least one armed reconnaissance sortie and two offensive bombing sorties in July 1948 and is shown carrying five bombs of three different weights. (Artwork by Peter Penev)

As of May and June 1948, the majority of AT-6s, T-6s and SNJs acquired by the SyAAF before the Palestine War seem to have been painted in BS381C/362 Mid-Stone and BS381C/226 Brunswick Green on upper surfaces and sides, with undersurfaces in BS381C/697 Light Admiralty Grey or a similar colour. The patterns in Brunswick Green differed from aircraft to aircraft, as did the size of roundels (applied in six positions) and fin flashes. Spinners – and sometimes wingtips – were usually painted in Dark Green, as in this case on serial number 205, but often left in Light Grey or bare metal. Most Syrian Texans/Harvards did not have any forward-firing machine guns, and this one did not have any installed in the rear cockpit, although the pintle was in its place. The aircraft is shown armed with a German-made SC100 bomb installed under the wing. (Artwork by Tom Cooper)

This North American AT-6 Texan was probably one of the examples secretly transferred from REAF stocks to Syria before the Palestine War and is why it was painted in in BS381C/361 Light Stone and BS381C/320 Light Brown on upper surfaces and sides, and BS381C/697 Light Admiralty Grey on undersurfaces. Instead of a serial number the aircraft was apparently named *al-Anqa'a* (*The Griffon*): this was applied in black on the right side of the engine cowling and white on the left. Sometime during the Palestine War, the spinner of this aircraft was painted in Dark Green (and, possibly also the wingtips), which became a form of 'quick visual identification' for Arab pilots. While having the bent cowling in front of the cockpit, it remains unclear if it was armed with anything other than a machine gun in the observer's position – this was either a Lewis gun (as shown), or a Vickers – in addition to at least two hardpoints for bombs under each wing. (Artwork by Tom Cooper)

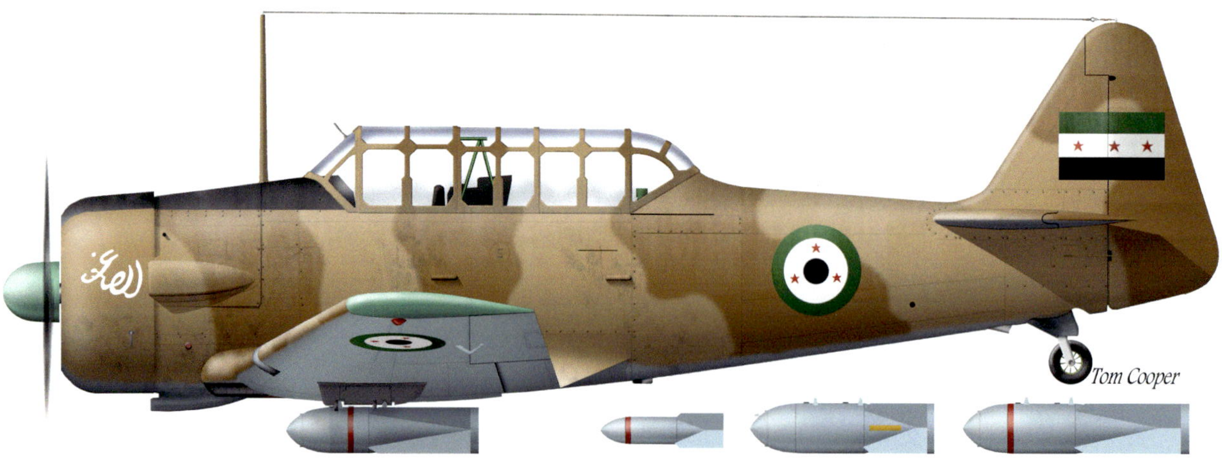

Another AT-6/T-6 Texan/Harvard probably transferred from REAF stocks to the SyAAF before the Palestine War was the example named *as-Sa'aq* (*Lightning*). Its top sides were painted in light stone and light brown, but while shown in Light Admiralty Grey on this artwork, the undersides might have been painted in a darker blue shade. When photographed in June 1948, *as-Sa'aq* had no machine gun installed in the rear cockpit, and only two underwing hardpoints, beneath which a range of German-made bombs of Second World War vintage (probably acquired from France) was put on display, including SC50 (lower centre), SC100 (shown as installed under the wing), and SD250 (lower right). Currently, there is no evidence that any of the ex-Egyptian Texans/Harvards in Syrian service were armed with forward-firing machine guns. (Artwork by Tom Cooper)

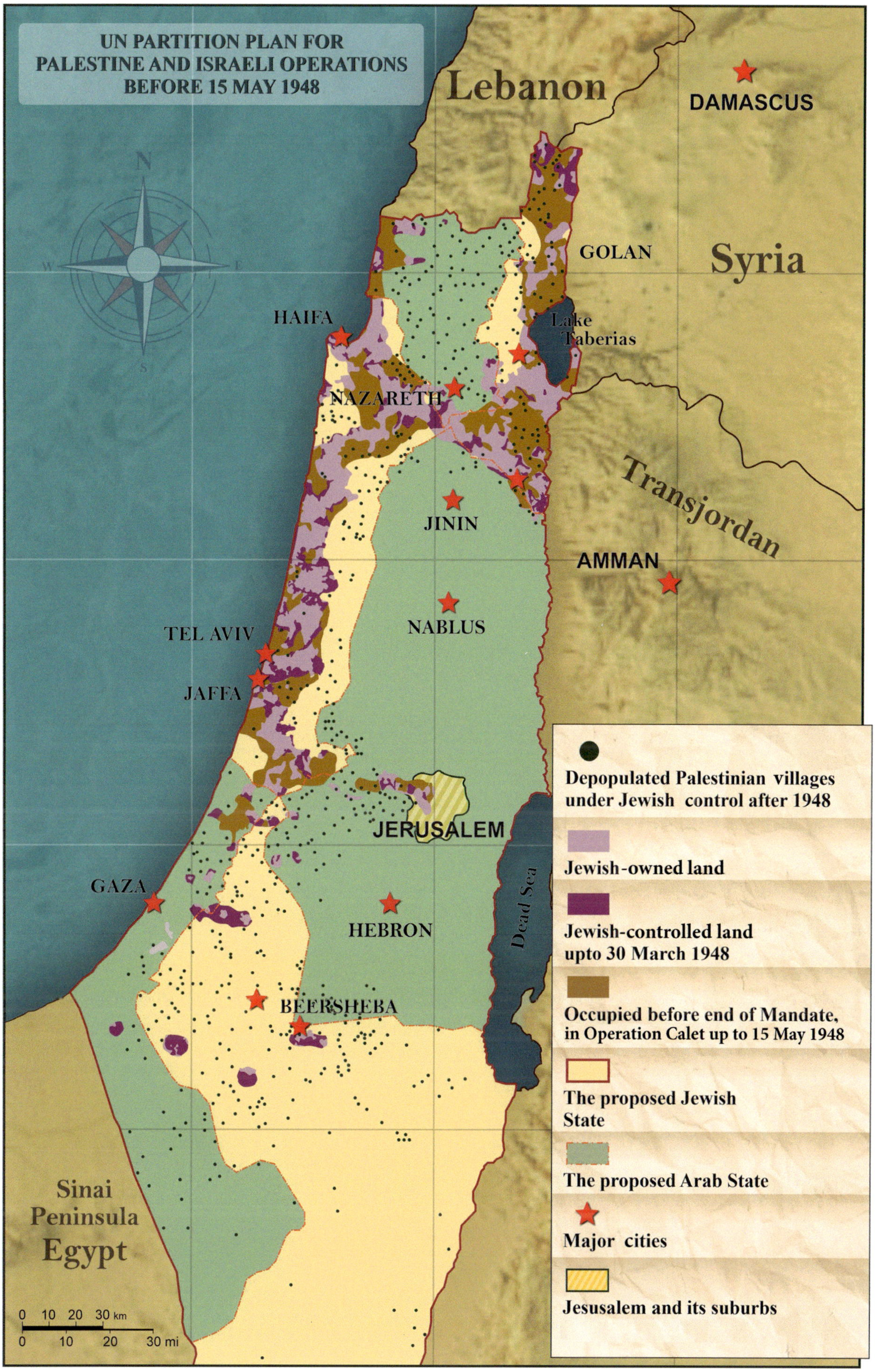

(Map by Anderson Subtil)

(Map by Anderson Subtil)

was now 7.30 in the morning. 'The inhabitants of this colony ran to see me and insulted me and spat in my face.'

About an hour later Irfan was bundled into a lorry with six soldiers who blindfolded him. They stopped at four other locations, each time the Egyptian pilot being spat at. 'At last, I reached Tel Aviv during a strong air attack. The lorry stopped near a big field and I could hear big explosions from bombs which seemed to be close to me....' After a siren sounded the all-clear the lorry moved on. Eventually Gamal Irfan was taken into a building and his blindfold was removed. He was in Yona Camp, a major training base for the *Haganah* situated not far from Tel Aviv port, where he remained for about a month before being sent to the main POW camp where he met Mahmud Barakat.

The raid by REAF C-47 'Dakota bombers' caused huge shock across Israel where the government announced that most of the casualties were civilians, calling the raid the 'first terror bombing in the Middle East since the Second World War' when Italian bombers had attacked Tel Aviv. During the afternoon pairs of Spitfires attacked the fortified settlements of Negba and Yad Mordechai in what Egyptian sources regard the REAF's first real close support mission in coordination with the Egyptian Army. Major Muhamad Kamil Siddiq cited what he called the Battle of Dayr Sunayd (named after the Palestinian village closest to Yad Mordechai) as particularly successful, first dropping high explosive bombs and incendiaries before strafing runs immediately prior to the direct assault by Egyptian troops.

However, there is disagreement between Egyptian and Israeli sources concerning REAF attacks on Yad Mordechai. The Egyptians often mention this target whereas some Israeli records suggest that there were only two air raids on Yad Mordechai, the first being in the afternoon of 18 May (or at 1815 hrs according to another source), the second being at 0715 hrs the following morning. An Egyptian news broadcast at 2200 hrs GMT on 18 May merely stated that; 'Heavy damage has been inflicted and several fires broke out.'

Some Israeli accounts state that a Spitfire was also forced down by Israeli groundfire from Yad Mordechai. Although there might be confusion between this incident and the downing of Gamal Irfan's Spitfire earlier in the day and about 45kms away, the evidence strongly suggests that the two REAF Spitfires were actually forced down on the 18th. The pilot of the aeroplane hit over Yad Mordechai reportedly made an emergency landing in or close to an Arab-held area and escaped. A memoir dating from this period recently came to light, written by the operational commanding officer in Kibbutz Yad Mordechai, named Munio. He wrote:

> At 1730 in the afternoon of May 18th, 1948, a solitary REAF Spitfire attacked the kibbutz. The pilot dropped two bombs on the kibbutz causing minor damage. Then he started strafing the kibbutz. After a few strafing dives the kibbutz defenders managed to hit the plane with their light weapons. The aircraft was seen leaving the kibbutz with smoke [or glycol coolant] in its trail. Later on, Arab sources stated that it crash-landed in Khan Yunis.

The Arab sources in question have not been identified, and if the pilot did reach the area of Khan Yunis, he was almost halfway to his home base at al-Arish.

In fact, this is likely to have been when REAF pilot Tahir Zaki was forced down for the first, though not the last, time. When interviewed by the author he recounted this adventure;

> The first time I was injured was when I was making a ground attack near Gaza [which lies 12kms south-west of Yad Mordechai]. I was hit by gunfire from the ground and had to make a forced landing between the Egyptian and Israeli lines. I got out of the aircraft and started to run towards the Egyptian positions. I remember I had a pistol, some water and some tins of nuts. That was when I saw an Israeli soldier in front of me. I shot at him with my pistol and continued running. Of course, I was quite fit in those days.

Not far away another pair of REAF Spitfires intercepted an Israeli Auster of the Negev Squadron at around 0715 hrs. The Auster had been sent to bomb an Egyptian motorised unit north of al-Majdal. Meanwhile Egyptian Spitfires had reportedly been attacking Israeli positions 'north of Gaza,' perhaps Yad Mordechai, though the location of the interception makes it more likely that the Egyptian pilots were returning from an attack in the Tel Aviv area. Caught after making the Auster's first bombing run, the Israeli pilot evaded the Spitfires' fire by popping in and out of clouds. The REAF fighters chased the Auster to Nir Am where Israeli anti-aircraft gunners claimed to have forced the Egyptians away as the Auster landed.

This first air interception of an Israeli aeroplane by the REAF clearly exposed the REAF's lack of air-gunnery training. In his frequently unreliable book *The Desert Hawks*, Leo Nomis stated that the Auster's bombs only released from one wing. While trying to release the others, the Israeli pilot was attacked by a Spitfire which 'came in so fast it overshot the Auster and, while the Spitfire was turning, the Israeli shook the stubborn bombs loose and dived for home. He frustrated the Egyptian with evasive tactics and when he got over Jaffa the Spitfire broke off pursuit.' No other versions of this event mention Jaffa, which lay well north of the Auster's target.

Elsewhere Iraqi Ansons were already hampered by the RIrAF's shortage of ammunition and other supplies. In fact, Iraqi Ansons are only known to have flown a few combat sorties during this first phase of the Palestine War. One was on 18 May 1948, when a pair led by Tallid al-Tikriti bombed the Israeli-held ex-RAF aerodrome at Ein Shemer with unknown results. After this mission, Iraqi ground crews worked for days to improvise new bombs and spares to make their aircraft ready for another mission.

For some reason the Ansons which bombed Ein Shemer have sometimes been described as Syrian 'heavy bombers.' According to this version, a pair of Ansons escorted by two Harvards appeared over Kfar Yona and Ein Shemer, far away from where SyAAF aircraft had previously operated. Israeli Intelligence initially identified the Ansons as Iraqi but the presence of Harvards which were assumed to be Syrian subsequently convinced them that all the aircraft were SyAAF. As far as is known there was no direct collaboration between the RIrAF at Mafraq in Transjordan and the SyAAF in Damascus, but this does not preclude the possibility of a joint Iraqi-Syrian mission against Ein Shemer and Kfar Yona. It is also possible that the single-engine aircraft were actually Iraqi Gladiators which remained at altitude to watch over the Ansons.

To further confuse the issue, Syrian High Command Communique No. 4, broadcast from Damascus at 2010 hrs GMT on 18 May, claimed that; 'Our planes brought down a plane over the Iraqi front.' This might indicate a confrontation south of Lake Tiberias, although it might also have been referring to the previous day. Nor was the difficulty of identifying unknown aeroplanes confined to observers on the ground. On 18 May the RAF's Nos. 32 and 208 Squadrons undertook a reconnaissance of the war-zone, and while flying along the Jordan Valley, the pilots of No. 32 Squadron saw a twin-engine aircraft heading southward. This they tentatively identified as a

Baltimore of unknown origin. It seems unlikely to have been one of the Iraqi Ansons and was perhaps a REAF C-47 Dakota flying between Egypt and Transjordan or Syria.

Further north the Israelis did not realise that the Lebanese force which crossed the frontier into Palestine had come to a halt. Here an Israeli attack upon the Nabi Yusha' police fortress during the night of 17–18 May seized this important location, after which Israeli forces began to consolidate their positions to block any Lebanese advance towards the Hula Valley.

Syrian or Palestinian troops man a machine gun position behind a sandbag barrier in northern Palestine, 1948. (Albert Grandolini collection)

19 MAY 1948

Ground Operations

On Wednesday 19 May, Ahmad Abd al-Aziz and his Egyptian Light Force entered Beersheba while the main Egyptian thrust pressed northward along the coastal road. Here the main battle for Yad Mordechai now began and after three hours desperate fighting one Egyptian company succeeded in seizing control of the sprawling settlement's southernmost fortified outpost. However, the other Egyptian companies were unable to exploit this success.

In the Jerusalem sector an Arab Legion task force led by a British officer, Major Slade, stormed the Shaikh Jarrah quarter, clearing the area of Israeli forces by 1130 hrs. This same force then linked up with Major al-Tal's Legionnaires inside the Old City, but because of strong Israeli resistance only the armoured car squadron reached the Old City at 1400 hrs. By now it was clear to General Glubb that his available forces were insufficient to establish a continuous line of defence, so the task force was pulled back to Shaikh Jarrah to await reinforcements, two additional companies arriving later that day, raising the force holding the area to about 500 men.

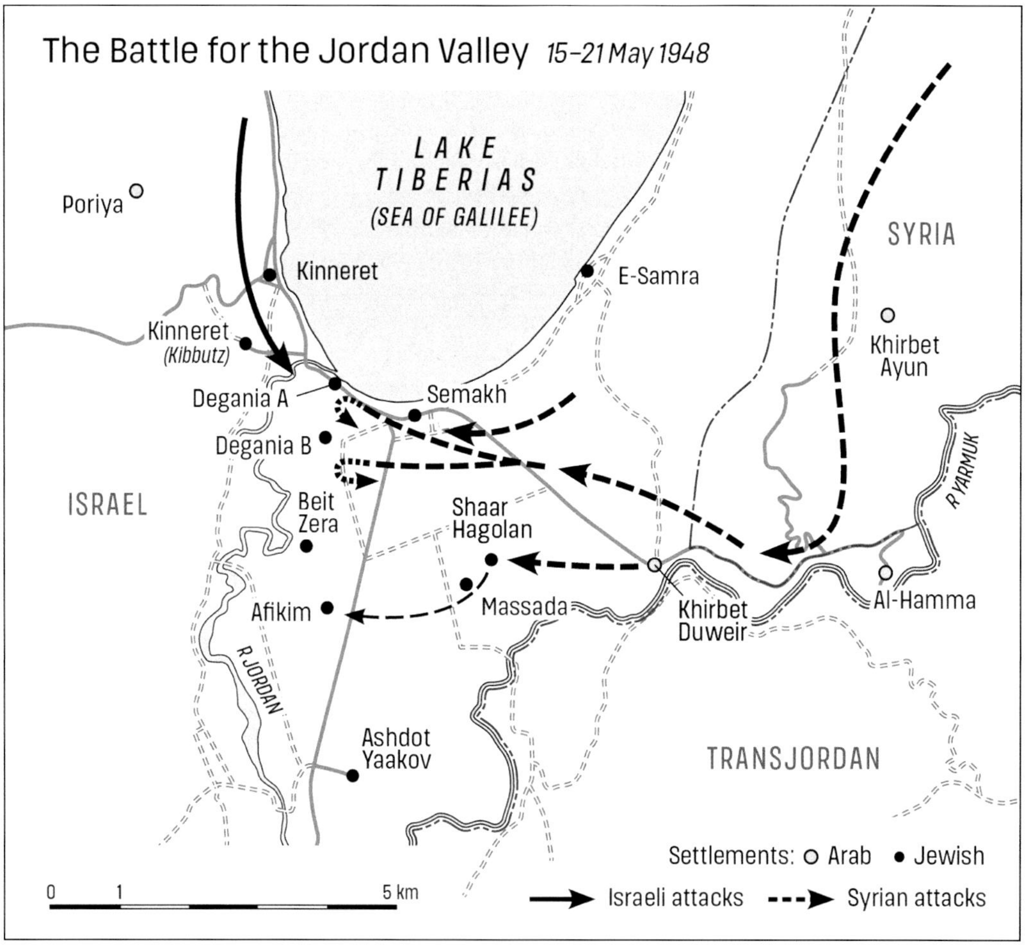

The Battle for the Jordan Valley, 15–21 May 1948. (Map by Paul Hewitt)

On the Syrian front, the second *Palmach* battalion had mounted a counterattack to retake Samakh during the night of 18–19 May, but this ended in failure. Meanwhile the defenders of the Massada and Shaar Hagolan settlements, whose morale had slumped following the loss of Samakh, withdrew from their positions and these two settlements had fallen into Syrian hands by morning. The gateway to the Jordan Valley seemed open. That same day the Iraqis, who were about to advance through Nablus towards Tulkarm, asked the Syrian Army to make a diversionary attack against the Degania settlements to protect the Iraqi right flank. Meanwhile, *Haganah* command sent Major Moshe Dayan to coordinate a defensive effort by reinforcements which were flown to the area and the troops already concentrated near the Deganias.

Air Operations

According to REAF sources, Egyptian aircraft made five further attacks, or an attack by five aircraft, against Yad Mordechai. According to some Israeli sources this location was only attacked once on the 19th, this being in the late afternoon around 1715 hrs. On the other hand, Meiri Ilan, the Israeli historian of Kibbutz Yad Mordechai, stated that the second of only two such raids took place at 0715 hrs on the morning of 19 May. All sources nevertheless agree that the raid was carried out by a pair of Spitfires armed with bombs and cannon. At around 1300 hrs on the 19th an Egyptian aircraft, probably a reconnaissance Lysander, dropped leaflets calling upon the Israeli defenders to surrender.

It was also reported that a single Egyptian aircraft attacked an Israeli Auster near Dayr Sunayd, though this might have been confused with a similar event the previous day. On the other hand, REAF Spitfire pilots were ordered to keep an eye open for Israeli light aircraft which were known to be bringing supplies, munitions and even personnel to besieged Israeli settlements. The Spitfires similarly monitored roads leading into these sprawling locations but could not maintain standing patrols. For example, on the 19th an Auster from the Tel Aviv Squadron flew low over Egyptian positions, its observer-gunner tossing out grenades and dropping a few small bombs. As one Israeli defender complacently observed; 'The effect fell short of precision but seemed satisfactorily demoralizing to the Arabs.' In reality it was no such thing.

Nevertheless, the number of Spitfires which had been lost or damaged as a result of groundfire convinced REAF HQ that future attacks should be made from a greater altitude. Quite when this order came into effect is unknown, but on 19th and 20 May the Tel Aviv electricity power station, along with petrol stores and harbour installations were again bombed while Egyptian fighters also strafed and bombed the substantial settlement of Negba. The latter was already taking on a strategic character because it was used as an Israeli army base area. In fact, the four days from 19th to 22 May would see a determined Egyptian attempt, not only to destroy Tel Aviv's harbour installations but also to damage industrial complexes which were known to be manufacturing equipment for Israeli forces.

On 19 May the day concluded with Cairo broadcasting Communique No. 7 from the Egyptian Ministry of Defence;

> The fires which broke out during yesterday's raids on the fortress of Negba could still be seen today. The fortifications of Bayt Hanun [the neighbouring Israeli settlement rather than the Arab village of that name] have been the main target of our Air Force today. Five successful consecutive raids have been launched, high explosive and incendiary bombs were dropped, reaching their objectives. Air operations were then suspended for some time on account of local bad weather conditions. In the afternoon.... our fighters attacked a Zionist armoured column near the fortress of Shdemot [just west of Nir Am].... Our bombers [a term which usually meant Dakota 'bombers'] resumed the bombing of Tel Aviv airport after it had been repaired by the Zionists. Hangers and runways received direct hits. Our dive bombers [meaning low-flying Spitfires] also raided the harbour and the wharves of Tel Aviv. All our aircraft returned safely to their bases [Refences to 'bases' in the plural might suggest that some bombers took off from Almaza].

Israeli accounts of the day merely stated that 'Enemy aircraft bombed the northern boundaries of Tel Aviv early this morning, and machine-gunned parts of the city.' The following day another Israeli broadcast confirmed that 'Enemy aircraft also dropped bombs at sunset on the 19th, mostly on the northern borders of Tel Aviv.'

Previously Mahmud Barakat had been given cigarettes, good food and treated with unexpected consideration by his Israeli guards, but around this time his experiences as a prisoner of war abruptly worsened, perhaps because the REAF attack on Tel Aviv's central bus station caused so many casualties. As he recalled;

> One day the door opened and some soldiers came in laughing. One of them was playing with the pistol in his hand, pushing it against my chest and behaving like a child who did not understand the consequences of his action. He even fired a shot into the ground, causing a fragment to go into my left knee. The blood flowed freely.

Subsequently an Israeli officer asked Barakat to identify this man, but the Egyptian refused. He was taken to the hospital which was already treating people who had been injured by REAF air strikes where, for his own safety, Barakat was put in a locked room with an

General Mukabri, Chief of Staff Syrian Arab Air Force, seen with a T-6 (see colour section for details). (Dr. David Nicolle collection)

armed guard at the door. Even so an Israeli soldier with a knife in his hand demanded to know where the Egyptian pilot was, one of this man's close relatives having been severely injured in an air attack.

Also on Wednesday 19 May, at least one Iraqi Anson bombed settlements just south of Lake Tiberias, in support of the Arab ground forces. Syrian Harvards were similarly active in support of the Syrian Army's 1st Brigade near Samakh. It was in the latter area that a Syrian Harvard pilot spotted an Israeli Auster and, instead of trying to shoot it down, followed the Israeli back to his base at Yavn'eel. He then returning with vital reconnaissance information which enabled the SyAAF to attack Yavn'eel later in the day. Peretz Grosser, the Israeli pilot in question, gave a different account of this confrontation. He claimed that the Syrian did try to shoot him down but, being foiled by Grosser's violent turns, instead followed the Israeli to Yavn'eel before turning for home. The subsequent raid by Syrian Harvards obliged the Israeli Galilee Squadron to move to a different and less convenient ex-RAF airfield at Mahanayim (now Rosh Pinna Airport). This would in turn be attacked by Syrian aircraft more than once, although the dispersed Israeli machines, four Austers and an Argus which were hidden beneath trees, escaped serious damage.

Syrian Army Communique No. 5, broadcast at 2050 hrs GMT on the 19th, exaggerated when it claimed that 'The Syrian Air Force destroyed two enemy aircraft near the settlement of Yavn'eel, and a third aircraft near the settlement of Ein Gev.' Nevertheless, the inexperienced SyAAF pilots may well have believed they inflicted such damage upon their enemies. The BBC monitor who listened to this broadcast from Damascus was also not entirely sure that he had heard the location Ein Gev correctly, this being in the narrow strip of Palestine along the south-eastern coast of the Lake Tiberias.

Late in the day, and during the night of 19–20 May, the Israeli Air Force resumed its offensive sorties, the first apparently being against armoured cars of the Arab Legion. Most such missions were in close support of Israeli ground forces, for example in the late evening of the 19th three aircraft of the Tel Aviv Squadron separately attempted to bomb Syrian positions at Samakh.

20 MAY 1948

Ground Operations

On the 20th and 21 May the Egyptian Army continued to thrust up the coastal road towards al-Majdal. Meanwhile the Egyptian assault upon Yad Mordechai was renewed. The sprawling Israeli settlement had by now been reinforced by *Palmach* forces from the Negev Brigade. This second Egyptian assault was again driven back with significant casualties on both sides, the Egyptian 2nd Battalion suffering 29 killed and 26 wounded while the Israeli defenders suffered 18 dead and 20 wounded.

To avoid another Egyptian failure, additional preparations had been carried out and the attacking force was supported by some armoured vehicles, including those described as captured Israeli tanks. Subsequently, Egyptian Communique No. 8 reported that;

> The battle here lasted ten hours. The importance of this colony is due to the fact that it is the main centre for supplying the southern Jewish colonies with men, arms and ammunition. It is also important from the military point of view by virtue of its commanding position over the movement of military forces from north to south since it is directly east of the road from Gaza to Tel Aviv. This colony has strong up-to-date fortifications. Moreover, it consists of a number of strong forts [concrete pill-boxes] surrounded by barbed wire and minefields extending over great distances. Our forces subjected this colony to the strongest artillery pounding, as well as to air bombardment.

Elsewhere during the morning, Major al-Tal of the Arab Legion led much of his unit towards Jerusalem's Old City while leaving an infantry company as a reserve in al-Tur. With Legionnaires approaching from the east, Colonel Shaltiel, the Israeli commander

A French-built Renault Char Léger Modèle 1935 light tank, dating from before the Second World War, captured by Israeli forces at Degania in northern Palestine in 1948. (Albert Grandolini collection)

in Jerusalem, launched a hurried assault to re-establish contact with the defenders of the Jewish Quarter.

On the Syrian front on 20 May, after an artillery bombardment, the Syrian 1st Brigade had begun its assault on the Degania settlements at 0430 hrs. The main attack targeted Degania Alef where the Syrian assault was spearheaded by five tankettes and armoured cars. It soon broke through the defences but the defenders destroyed several vehicles with anti-tank guns and PIAT anti-tank weapons. The surviving tankettes withdrew and an infantry company, some distance behind these vehicles, was forced to halt in citrus groves several hundred metres from the settlement.

At noon, the Syrians pulled back from Degania Alef and, redirecting their effort southward, the Syrians next concentrated upon Degania Bet but had no better luck. After two unsuccessful attacks the Syrians ran out of ammunitions and abandoned any further attempt. Instead, the 1st Brigade moved north again. Moreover, the Iraqi advance towards Tulkarm had exposed the Syrians' right flank, obliging the Syrian commanders to withdraw their 1st Brigade for reorganisation before committing it once again in the Finger of Galilee. Here it would be joined by two ALA battalions and, together with the Lebanese force, the Syrians and ALA planned to advance towards Safad. The battered condition of the 1st Brigade nevertheless made this impossible, so the Syrian thrust was shifted to an area north of Lake Tiberias near the Jisr Banat Ya'qub (the Bridge of Jacob's Daughters), while an ALA battalion replaced the Syrian 1st Brigade south of Lake Tiberias. Except for a sporadic artillery bombardment of Israeli settlements in the Hula Valley, the Syrian front then remained quiet for two weeks.

Unfortunately, some Israeli forces now returned to the brutal series of actions, regarded by many as war crimes, which had characterised many pre-Independence Zionist paramilitary units, four such incidents being recorded during the night of 20–21 May 1948.

Air Operations

The intensity of REAF activity remained relatively high, and from 20th to 22 May Egyptian Spitfires attacked Gan Yavne, Gedera, Negba, Nir Am, Dorot and Gvar'am. Dakota bombers struck Tel Aviv's main power station, oil storage tanks, various workshops and a chemical plant, their escorting Spitfires attacked the port where one strafed the Polish freighter *Levant*, wounding a member of its crew. Egyptian Communique No. 9 broadcast from Cairo at 2345 hrs GMT on the 20th was quite specific, stating that; 'Our bombers this morning raided stores, munitions factories, an oxygen factory and oil installations south-east of Tel Aviv, direct hits causing numerous explosions. The planes repeated the attack [probably referring to subsequent attacks during the afternoon], causing further fires.'

Tel Aviv's version broadcast at 0730, stated that 'An earlier report stated that at 0530 local time, an enemy aircraft appeared over Tel Aviv and dropped a few bombs, causing no damage nor loss of life.' At 2030 another broadcast reported that; 'Enemy aircraft again raided Tel Aviv this afternoon; bombs were dropped in some parts of the town. An enemy aircraft was shot down.'

There is no evidence of an Egyptian aeroplane being lost but a British RAF machine was damaged. A section of No. 32 Squadron Spitfires from Ramat David had been carrying out reconnaissance over southern Palestine and near Tel Aviv one received a bullet through one wing. Another RAF section was greeted by light anti-aircraft fire in the vicinity of Aqir.

The REAF was also called upon to 'soften up' a line of fortified settlements east of al-Majdal, in preparation for future Egyptian Army assaults. As part of this, according to Egyptian Communique No. 9; 'Our aircraft carried out two successful raids against the Jewish colony of Negba [confirmed by Israeli sources], where heavy bombing of the target was maintained.' Furthermore; 'Our planes opened fire on a convoy of vehicles on the road near Rehovot.' The latter were probably reinforcements heading towards the front north of al-Majdal or to Israeli settlements east of the coastal road.

Another sequence from the filming of *A Girl from Palestine*, showing REAF Spitfire Mk V serial number ER603, taxying prior to take-off from Hilwan. Notable is the very dark underwing surface and two training bombs. It is unclear if this aircraft saw combat operations or was held back at Hilwan for advanced training of additional pilots. (Dr. David Nicolle collection)

REAF ground crew taking a trolley of bombs to a Spitfire at al-Arish during the Palestine War. (Dr. David Nicolle collection)

Arab aircraft were similarly active over the eastern front, though their identity remains unclear, a broadcast from Tel Aviv at 2030 hrs GMT stating that; 'Ramat Rahel was also bombed; no casualties occurred.' This kibbutz on the southern outskirts of Jerusalem was cut off by Arab forces during the Palestine War and the aeroplane or aeroplanes involved might have been Iraqi or Egyptian. At 2215 hrs GMT a Syrian Army communique, repeated from Beirut, stated that; 'Our Air Force bombed enemy concentrations on the Kfar Him [unidentified] road, scoring direct hits and destroying cars. Our planes raided the settlements of Kinneret and Yavn'eel and machine-gunned the defeated enemy. They also raided the settlement of Haraawah [unidentified] and set in on fire.'

This effort meant that Syrian aircraft did little or nothing to support the Syrian Army's ground assaults against the Degania settlements whereas Israeli aircraft renewed their bombing campaign during the night of 20–21 May, targeting Syrian positions. According to Israeli sources, intercepted Syrian radio messages indicated that a lack of air support was undermining moral amongst Syrian troops. One radio conversation reportedly said; 'Enemy aircraft overhead.' 'We have been promised by HQ the arrival of Iraqi planes, do not worry.' 'Two of our guns were damaged.' 'Do not worry, our aircraft will soon join the battle.' In the event, Iraqi air support to the Syrians was minimal.

On the Israeli side, the first Avia S-199 – Czech-built versions of the Messerschmitt Bf 109 – arrived on board a large transport aircraft on 20 May. It would be another two weeks before they were operational and, being fully aware of the menace they posed, the REAF put considerable effort into locating the base from which Avia S-199s would operate. Meanwhile, other Israeli aircraft remained active after dark and during the night of 20–21 May a Dragon Rapide, a Bonanza and Arguses targeted the unused Gaza airfield, a reported Egyptian Army HQ in Gaza railway station, and the village of Shu'fat north of Jerusalem.

21 MAY 1948

Ground Operations

By now Arab and Israeli forces were both seriously overstretched. The Egyptian Army Headquarters in Cairo was also under mounting political pressure, not least from King Faruq himself, and on 21 May General al-Muwawi was ordered to take full control of al-Majdal. But because Yad Mordechai still threatened his main line of communications, al-Muwawi only committed the 1st Infantry Battalion to advance along a subsidiary road, al-Majdal being entered without resistance late in the evening. Here the terrified inhabitants greeted the soldiers with almost hysterical joy.

Israeli forces were themselves besieged in the settlements of Gat and Gal On, east of Falujah, but of greater concern to the Egyptians was the large settlement of Negba. It was not surrounded and could be used as a base from which to attack the Arabs' east–west communications. Nearby Arab-held Iraq Suwaidan and its formidable police fortress not only controlled the lateral road between al-Majdal and Hebron, but dominated the Israeli supply road to the Negev through the ethnically cleansed Palestine villages of Kawkaba, al-Hulaiqat and Burair. Nevertheless, the Egyptians did not have sufficient troops to take over Iraq Suwaidan and its police fort until the 24th when, having received reports about a nearby concentration of Israeli forces, the Egyptian commander sent a unit eastward to consolidate this vital position. Only now could General al-Muwawi seriously hope to isolate southern Israeli forces in the Negev, this being done more or less completely during the early days of June. To the south-east, the Muslim Brethren and Egyptian Light Force under Colonel Abd al-Aziz reached Bethlehem where they linked up with King Abdullah's Arab Legion. As a result, a huge area of southern Palestine became the responsibility of a force of poorly trained but religiously motivated volunteers supported by a smaller number of Egyptian regulars.

To the north, Iraqi forces were instructed by King Abdullah of Transjordan, their nominal C-in-C, to replace Arab Legion and ALA units in a triangle of territory between Jinin, Tulkarm and Nablus. Another Iraqi regiment was meanwhile on its way to join Iraqi forces in Palestine as they concentrated in the area of Nablus. These moves were

Palestinian tracked artillery in 1948. The three-colour camouflage scheme appears to have been typical of ALA armoured vehicles. (Albert Grandolini collection)

A water tower at Beerot-Yitzak, similar to the one attacked by Tahir Zaki in Yad Mordechai. (Dr. David Nicolle collection)

One of the five Westland Lysanders (serial number 504) which are known to have served at the front during the Palestine War, seen here with an Italian Macchi delivery pilot seated on the wheel fairing at al-Arish. (Dr. David Nicolle collection)

in preparation for a renewed assault upon Israeli defences. Sadly, on the Israeli side another war crime against the Palestinian Arab population allegedly took place on 21 May.

Air Operations

On 21 May REAF Spitfires were back in action, hitting Gan Yavne, Genera (Gedera?) and Negba, along with airstrips at Nir Am, Gvar'am and Dorot. Other Egyptian aircraft, probably Spitfires, hit Aqir and Lydda airfields as well as the nearby railway line. The attack on Aqir appears to have been particularly effective, hitting a hanger and reportedly killing a number of Israeli Air Force personnel. Following an attack upon an unspecified ex-RAF landing ground just south of Ramlah – probably referring to Aqir – Egyptian Communique No. 10 claimed that the REAF 'destroyed fifteen lorries loaded with ammunition as well as other goods stored in the airfield.' The communique concluded with the emphatic statement that no Egyptian aeroplanes were lost this day.

The REAFs offensive against military, logistical and industrial targets in Tel Aviv continued with Dakotas bombing factories on the outskirts of the city, there being no mention of escorting Spitfires. Later in the day Egyptian Official Communique No. 10 stated that; 'Our bombers raided steel factories near Tel Aviv and scored direct hits. Oxygen factories east of Jaffa were also raided, causing several explosions and fires from which long columns of smoke rose.' For its part, the Israeli *Haganah* issued a communique which claimed that 'Tel Aviv and suburbs were bombed by enemy aircraft this morning, but no damage was caused.'

REAF raids on Yad Mordechai now appear to have paused as Negba became a more important target. Nevertheless, most REAF sorties were against approaching reinforcements. At noon an Egyptian armoured column advanced against Negba. The settlement's water tank was also hit, Negba's commander Yishak Dubno being killed while directing anti-aircraft fire, and it seems likely that both the water tank and Dubno were struck by gunfire from REAF Spitfires which were giving close support to the Egyptian Army assault.

Mention of an Israeli settlement's water tank being targeted brings to mind Egyptian Spitfire pilot Tahir Zaki's recollection of a similar, or perhaps the same, incident. However, it is possible that Tahir Zaki's memory was at fault when he told the author that he smashed a settlement's water tower, after which that settlement soon fell to the Egyptian Army. Negba never fell, but Yad Mordechai did, although Israeli sources deny that the strafing of Yad Mordechai's water tower had significant impact upon its abandonment on 24 May. When interviewed by the author, the now aged Tahir Zaki recalled that the Israelis had four fortified settlements near the Egyptian frontier. In his words;

> The Army Command could not understand why the soldiers could not capture them. We pilots saw a hill surrounded by barbed wire with trenches behind this. The place also had a water tank, which had fortifications around it and from which people could shoot down on our troops. I attacked this water tank with bombs and destroyed its defences. I asked General Mu'wawi to let me attack its water tower with bombs again. I thought this would reduce Egyptian casualties in their next attack.

Perhaps attacks on the two water towers were conflated in the old pilot's memory.

Meanwhile, according to an Israeli source, a Westland Lysander bombed Negba, perhaps as a secondary aspect of what was primarily a reconnaissance sortie. Normally these slow and archaic aeroplanes were used for photo-reconnaissance or for dropping leaflets calling upon Israeli outposts to surrender. According to Israeli historian Meiri Ilan, the first attack on Negba by a Lysander was on 21 May, with Spitfires also attacking on the same day. Other Israeli sources state that two Egyptian Spitfires attacked a convoy of five armoured cars near Nir Am during the morning of 21 May. Egyptian Communique No. 10 merely stated that; 'Further raids were carried out by our Air Force against the Jewish colonies of Negba and Shdimuth [Shdemot], causing damage and fires.' Communique No. 10 further reported that 'Our aircraft scored several direct hits on a train of twenty-five carriages east of Caesarea and put it out of action.' This was probably a target of opportunity when REAF Spitfires were searching for the illusive Israeli Avia S-199s.

After the tragic events over Ramat David on the following day, there was an initial report that the first Egyptian aeroplane seen over this RAF aerodrome was a Lysander, but it unlikely that a REAF Lysander ranged this far north. It is nevertheless possible that the first Egyptian pilot to report seeing unknown fighters on the ground at Ramat David did so on 21 May. It has also been suggested that Arab intelligence reports, relying on observers on the ground, raised the possibility that the British fighters at Ramat David may have been Israeli.

The previous day's lack of SyAAF or RIrAF support for Syrian troops did not mean they remained inactive. In fact, on 21 May Syrian Harvards attacked Israeli forces south of Lake Tiberias while Iraqi Ansons bombed Israeli settlements on the western bank of the River Jordan and at a strategic crossroads near Baysan in support of Iraqi Army movements. A report from Baghdad, broadcast from Damascus at 1845 hrs GMT, stated that; 'Iraqi and Syrian aircraft raided Jewish colonies in the north-eastern sector.' Syrian Army Communique No. 7, repeated by Egyptian radio, said of operations over the previous 24 hours; 'Our artillery, in conjunction with the Air Force, has pounded three other Jewish colonies, causing big fires.' Israeli sources confirmed that Syrian Harvards attacked vehicle concentrations along with Jewish settlements at Kinneret and Yavn'eel, the latter being the site of an important Israeli aerodrome. Apparently, Syrian aircraft also dropped leaflets over some Jewish settlements.

Elsewhere, an Israeli broadcast report at 2030 merely stated that; 'Shots were fired from an unidentified aircraft on a police station in the settlement of Marawa [unidentified] during the afternoon.' This broadcast also noted that Kfar Shefat north-west of Jerusalem (presumably meaning Shu'fat north-east of the Holy City) had been bombed by Israeli aircraft on the 20th. For its part, the Israeli Air Force announced that its aeroplanes had bombed military objectives in the Gaza area. Other Israeli aircraft attacked enemy concentrations, probably from the Arab Legion, at a village south-east of Jerusalem identified as 'Apak.' This might have been when the two Arguses of the Tel Aviv Squadron bombed the Arab neighbourhood of Shaikh Jarrah.

To the north, within the British declared Haifa Enclave, the RAF at Ramat David lost one aeroplane in an unusual accident on the 21st when the throttle of a No. 32 Squadron Spitfire jammed open when taking off. The machine hit the ground and cartwheeled twice although its pilot, Flying Officer Sloan, emerged with relatively minor injuries.

22 MAY 1948

On Saturday 22 May the UN draft resolution calling for a ceasefire was at last passed, the text having been amended to meet Israeli objections. Israel had been under serious pressure from the regular Arab forces, while the Israeli army desperately needed time to absorb the men and the arms which were flowing into the country. Consequently, the Israeli government welcomed the four weeks truce proposed at the UN. In contrast, the Arab League's Political Committee only agreed to this ceasefire if the Security Council prohibited immigration by those they described as 'recruits for the Jewish forces,' along with banning Israel's importation of military material. These Arab conditions were of course unacceptable to Israel, so the Arab League refused to accept a truce, maintaining that it would merely enable Israel to strengthen its position.

Ground Operations

After the first Israeli line of defence running from Beersheba to Gaza had crumbled in the face of the Egyptian advance, a second defence line had been established with forward positions around Kfar Warburg on the 'middle road' some 13kms north of Falujah. Many of the natural features used in this new line had earlier been unsuccessfully used by the Ottoman Army during the First World War, but the Egyptians lacked the organisation, equipment and numbers enjoyed by the British just over 30 years earlier. In fact, the Egyptian Expeditionary Force had reached as far as it could and was hardly in a condition to advance further. Instead, it consolidated its gains while Israeli forces attempted to disrupt Egyptian dispositions.

Although the main Egyptian Army front was now largely static, the Egyptian Light Force under Colonel Aziz continued to move forward, having linking up with the Arab Legion near Bethlehem. Meanwhile, a detachment from the Egyptian main body replaced Aziz's volunteers in al-Auja, then followed in their footsteps to Beersheba. When these additional forces arrived, Colonel Aziz deployed them in defence of a huge area, with one detachment in al-Auja, another in Bir 'Asluj and the rest in Beersheba. Here they would, for a while, enjoy a relatively quiet war.

With heavy fighting still going on in Jerusalem, General Glubb decided to replace his hastily assembled existing assorted companies by a single tactical unit. The 3rd Regiment in the Nablus area was the only one available and after arriving in Jerusalem early on 22 May it launched a two-pronged assault. The first was against Israeli positions in the area southeast of the Shaikh Jarrah quarter, subsequently known as the Mandelbaum Gate. The second was to target the Notre Dame Monastery which had been converted into a fortified Israeli position threatening the partly Christian Arab Musrara quarter to the north. However, because the regiment commander did not have experienced guides to lead his Bedouin companies, some lost their way in the narrow streets of the Old City, causing this assault to be postponed until the following day. Sadly, the night of 22–23rd also witnessed yet another alleged war crime by Israeli forces against Palestinian Arabs.

Air Operations

Apart from the catastrophe which would take place over Ramat David (see below), three other REAF actions were reported on 22 May. The first was in support of an Egyptian Army artillery and tank bombardment of the Israeli settlement of Negba. This was probably the raid led by Abd al-Rahman Inan which had been diverted from its primary intended target of Ramat David early in the morning. According to a broadcast from Cairo later in the day, Egyptian 'bombers' had also attacked 'enemy armoured detachments near the settlement of Rishon-le-Zion.' Cairo similarly reported an attack on an electricity plant and 'heavy factories' south-east of Tel Aviv. In fact, the raids within and south-east of Tel Aviv may have been one and same or have been closely associated.

Saturday 22 May 1948 was otherwise a day of disaster for the REAF, caused by a lack of information about existing British military positions within the Haifa Enclave, along with poor weather conditions, poor maps and poor navigation on the part of Egyptian pilots. The catastrophe was also caused by the REAF's absolute determination to find and destroy the Israelis' new fighter force before it could cause a serious threat.

An account of the Ramat David incident which has not received the attention it deserves is that of *Qa'id Sirb* Abd al-Rahman Inan, the pilot who was captured during the last REAF attack on Ramat David. He described this dramatic episode;

> At 3 o'clock [0300 hrs Cairo time] a soldier entered my tent to wake up myself and Qa'id Asrab Nasr al-Din Zaghlul. We got up and put on our clothes in the dark, then went to the Operations Room where, after a few minutes, six pilots assembled. They awaited orders from me because I was the formation leader. I told them that our reconnaissance aircraft had found that the Zionists had assembled an air force near Haifa.... We had to destroy them today and that this would change the course of the war for a long time.... Later we discussed details concerning bombs, ammunition, communications, the way we should attack, and so on.

Six aeroplanes were to take part, flown by Abd al-Rahman Inan, Muhammad Nasr al-Din Zaghlul, Tutmos Kamil Ibrahim Gibra'il, Abd al-Karim Muharram, perhaps al-Qarmuti and perhaps Tahir Zaki.

Inan recalled that he regarded this mission as being like his previous 16 sorties of the Palestine War;

> I started my engine, assembled the flight and looked for enemies in the sky, knowing that it was a matter of life or death who attacked whom first. Before daylight everything was ready, but the weather report was not good. There was dense cloud [probably above 3,000 metres] and fog covered the airbase so that we could see no further than 100 metres. So, we had to wait.

In fact, the six pilots got out of their machines. While they waited, Inan watched and admired the base's ground crews hard at work like a tireless hive of bees. The mist then lifted, the pilots returned to their cockpits and took off with their full bomb loads. Inan's account continued; 'After half an hour I found that there was too much cloud and we could not identify our target, so I was ordered to attack a settlement in the Negev desert [probably Negba]. I chose one [position] that was bombarding a [nearby] Arab village with mortars.' After returning from this mission, Inan learned that *Qa'id Asrab* Zaghlul had not heard the order to divert and had therefore gone on to attack the original target alone. 'All of us were now waiting for him and were hoping that he did not find the target, which would mean that we would lose the element of surprise.' However, Zaghlul did hit Ramat David at around 0530 hrs, according to official Egyptian sources, before returning to al-Arish. Inan was immediately ordered by Muhammad Sidqi Mahmud al-Milaigy and the commander of al-Arish airbase to take the remaining five by now refuelled Spitfires and attack the same target before the enemy could move his aeroplanes. In fact, only three machines were ready while two needed a few more minutes before they could take-off.

The second strike was therefore divided into two waves and the base commander told Inan to select the pilots for each. Tutmos Kamil Gibra'il said he was ready, as did Abd al-Karim Muharram although he had already taken part in the first sortie;

REAF pilots in the briefing room at al-Arish synchronise their watches before a mission. Muhammad Abu Zaid is second from the left. (Dr. David Nicolle collection)

The Spitfire LF.Mk 9 serial number 642 of the REAF, here with part of a mission list for all the fighter-bombers of the Tactical Air Force visible on the far left, now with complete national markings and a large serial number on the rear fuselage (for other details, see the colour section). The aircraft was photographed at Hilwan aerodrome during the filming of *A Girl from Palestine*. (Dr. David Nicolle collection)

Two REAF Spitfire pilots based at Hilwan during the summer of 1948, perhaps as advanced instructors, with an Egyptian Supermarine Spitfire V during the filming of *A Girl from Palestine*. (Dr. David Nicolle collection)

> We did not drink any tea after we arrived [at the aircraft, presumably because they were in a hurry, although drinking tea immediately before take-off was normal practice in the REAF]. I asked the Commander, who would follow me with Zaghlul? He looked behind him to Qa'id Asrab al-Qarmuti who was heading for the toilet and cafeteria and said to himself, 'Let him have something to eat'. He then looked towards Tayyar Awal Sa'ad Sadiq [al-Duwayni] and it was then that Death selected his victims.

Another aerial view of Ramat David air base. (Photo by R. Bowie via Brian Cull)

As they approached their target, Inan tried to contact Tutmos and Muharram but they did not answer, their radio communication apparently not working. However, their plan had already been agreed;

> I started the attack by diving on a big aircraft hangar, and I put this hangar in the middle of the bombsight then dropped the bombs over the target. Then I turned to attack it again with guns, and I saw a fire-truck going towards the hangar to fight the fires. A moment later I saw the bombs of pilot Tutmos hit the hangar and explode amongst aircraft around the hangar, destroying them all [as Inan believed]. I attacked the target with guns twice.

British versions of the attacks on Ramat David were written after the event, when the participants had sorted out their conflicting recollections and are probably not as reliable as Abd al-Rahman Inan's account. One official RAF version stated that two REAF Spitfires came over Ramat David at low altitude at 0600 hrs (more correctly 0610); the first dropping two 250lb bombs on the dispersal area and setting fire to two RAF Spitfires, after which the second did some ineffective strafing. In fact, there was only one Egyptian Spitfire, flown by *Qa'id Asrab* Zaghlul who attacked twice.

A British Foreign Office account stated that there were separate attacks, the second and third actually being the two waves of one mission, and that these took place between 0600 and 0930 local time. The first was by a single Spitfire and at first the British were unsure of the attackers' identity, so the base commander sent up a standing patrol of Spitfires while the aerodrome's anti-aircraft defences were put on high alert. The second attack was at 0900 and the third at 0930, these destroying one Dakota and damaged five others. Two RAF officers and one airman had been killed and three men wounded. By the end of the third attack, according to this British Foreign Office account, four or possibly five Egyptian Spitfires had been shot down; the latter figure agreeing with the report broadcast by Cairo Radio and admitted in several official and unofficial Egyptian sources. A further important point is that the third attack, which was in reality the second wave of the second attack, took off from al-Arish well after the first wave of this second attack had been expected to return. Its pilots must therefore have known that something serious had happened to their predecessors.

According to Ali Muhammad Labib's semi-official history of the Egyptian Air Force, after the base commander at al-Arish was informed that the enemy's fighter base had been found, 'a further five Spitfires of the total eight parked at al-Arish took off to follow up the [first] attack on Ramat David.' Labib's reference to eight Spitfires being available at that time perhaps meant that only eight were currently serviceable, two or three having already been lost to Israeli ground fire.

According to British sources, REAF Spitfires attacked Ramat David for the second time around 0745 hrs. The main hanger was hit, a Spitfire FR18 and a C-47 transport being destroyed. However, British sources state that one Egyptian Spitfire was damaged by anti-aircraft fire while a second was shot down by British fighters.

At 0915 hrs another two Egyptian Spitfires 9s attempted a third attack, but these were intercepted by four of the RAF's more advanced Spitfires FR18s, one Egyptian Spitfire being shot down while the other was damaged and subsequently crashed. These catastrophic events, during which three Egyptian pilots were killed and one taken prisoner, were a serious blow to the small Tactical Air Force based at al-Arish. Subsequently the Egyptian authorities claimed to have been told by the British that the RAF would have left the Haifa Enclave by this time.

One of the Egyptian REAF Supermarine Spitfire 9s forced down within Israeli-held territory during the Palestine War. Its identity is unknown but the damage to the top of the cockpit indicates that it had turned over when it crashed. (Dr. David Nicolle collection)

The Israelis attempted, with limited success, to make use of what remained of any Arab aircraft which fell into their hands. Here part of the rear fuselage of a REAF Spitfire, along with what might be the centre-section of another and parts of more than one wing are seen beneath camouflage netting, probably in northern Israel. (Dr. David Nicolle collection)

The first attack was witnessed by a rather hung-over Flying Officer Tim McElhaw of No. 208 Squadron who had only got to bed at 01.00 hrs the previous night. He awoke at five to six and went outside to relieve himself, heard an aircraft and looked up. 'Then I saw an aeroplane diving towards the aerodrome and reckoned it must be an early morning patrol, that I hadn't heard about, doing a beat-up for fun – that was until I saw a couple of bombs unhitch from the wings and continue down.' McElhaw's colleague, Flying Officer Bowie continued the story; 'We threw on some clothes and raced for the aircraft which were covered in smoke and flames and exploding ammunition. As everyone headed for the aircraft, another Spitfire [actually the same machine] appeared on a strafing run but was so high we couldn't see his markings and he did no damage.'

Other British sources record that the solitary Spitfire circled Ramat David aerodrome a number of times before attacking. Four No. 208 Spitfires scrambled but were too late to catch this Egyptian, now known to have been Nasr al-Din Zaghlul. According to these British accounts, at around 0745 hrs three REAF Spitfires again attacked the aerodrome, bombing a hangar and a scrapped Spitfire, before destroying a Dakota with cannon and machine gun fire, seven other RAF planes being damaged.

The first RAF standing patrol had gone to investigate the Israelis' firing on an RAF Proctor near Haifa but soon returned. Another standing patrol of two Spitfires from No. 208 Squadron remained in the area of Ramat David and by the time Inan and his colleagues made their attack, this patrol had been alerted. Four RAF Spitfires attacked the three Egyptians, one being shot down, one hitting the ground while taking evasive action, and one was brought down by anti-aircraft fire. At least one British source maintained that an Egyptian pilot was captured and then handed over to the Israelis, whereas Inan's own account shows that he came down within Israeli-controlled territory and was captured by Israeli troops.

Further British sources indicate that the second wave led by *Qa'id Sirb* Inan attacked Ramat David from the north which suggest that the Egyptians had probably followed the coast of Palestine around the peninsula of Mount Carmel, over Haifa and down the Jezreel Valley. Another suggested that the Egyptian Spitfires had followed three RAF Dakotas, two from No. 78 Squadron and one from No. 70 Squadron, which accounted for their approaching from the north, but this is not mentioned by Abd al-Rahman Inan.

Lawrence Fellows, an airman of No. 32 Squadron, stated that; 'Two enemy aircraft dived out of the sun, guns blazing.' At that time of day, the sun was low in the south-east – the opposite direction to Haifa. Fellows continued; 'The enemy aircraft was.... pursued by one of our aircraft, which soon shot him down. The second enemy aircraft, which had dodged and evaded our other fighter for a few minutes, dropped its two bombs, one of which landed only a couple of yards from a Dakota.' Flying Officer Bowie was part of the RAF standing patrols and recalled being south of the aerodrome when he saw a cloud of smoke;

> We were called up by the tower to say they had been attacked from the north.... We dived in over the airfield and intercepted a Spitfire with Egyptian markings. We spoke to Sqn. Ldr. Ambrose, who told us to shoot him down – which we did – whereupon another Spitfire appeared, which we chased at ground level off to the south. Geoff [Cooper] got in several bursts, which raised a great deal of dirt and the last one hit fair and square and the aircraft disappeared in a cloud of dust.

It is difficult to make these versions of events fit with that of Abd al-Rahman Inan who eventually came down about 15kms away, near the southern end of the Mount Carmel hills.

The REAF Spitfire downed by ground fire was said to have come down in hills to the south. Later in the day, after the REAF's third and final attack, some men from the aerodrome went in search of the crashed Spitfires, one of which was found between three and five kilometres to the south. It was said to be the first of those brought down by RAF Spitfires, rather than by the RAF Regiment's ground fire.

Abd al-Rahman Inan recalled that while making his third attack run;

> I felt as if I was in danger, so I looked behind my aircraft and saw two Spitfires shooting at me from a distance of 100 metres. At first I was not sure whether they might have been friends, but then I saw that their propeller hubs were red, not green like on our aircraft [not all REAF Spitfires had green or green and white spinners, but certainly none had red spinners], so I was convinced they were the enemy, but I could not warn my colleagues because our communications were not working [one of his colleagues may already have been shot down, although Inan would have been unaware of this].
>
> I decided to try and draw the enemy away towards the mountains [Mount Carmel] and out to the sea. I flew very low to make the enemy leave my friends alone. Also, the colour of my aircraft was like that of the sea, in which case it would be difficult for the enemy to hit me.... I turned around to face them and recklessly flew between them and saw the insignia of the British RAF on the fuselage of the aircraft. I tried to take a chance by running away so I dived steeply but I found that they were still behind me. They were better than my aircraft [a Spitfire 9]. It was stronger type [Spitfire 18s]. One of them started to shoot at me but before it started [to hit] I went to the right to avoid his guns but then the second aircraft hit me and shot my engine and right wing with 20mm bullets, one of which exploded near my face about 30cm away....
>
> Then the engine stopped and there was heavy white smoke pouring out and my aircraft start to drop towards the ground. The right wing swung around because the aileron was destroyed; I feared that the control wires might have been severed and that I would lose control of my aircraft [In fact, this damage resulted in Inan heading back towards Ramat David]. So, I quickly pulled the stick to the left and back to bring the tail down so that I would not hit the ground so hard. It was impossible for me to bale out because I was only 160 metres from the ground [over the rugged Carmel range]....
>
> At that point an aeroplane came and shot at me again, hitting my machine, smashing the windscreen and destroying my engine. The smoke became thicker and thicker and I was descending ever faster towards the ground.

Through the smoke Inan could see hilltops all around, so he pulled back the cockpit hood only to find that he was heading straight for a mountain surrounded by gullies;

> I gathered all my strength and pulled back the control column and prayed that I would not pass out before I hit ground. An aeroplane shot at me a third time with cannon-fire, and that was when my aircraft hit the ground – but I was still alive. The nose and right wing hit the ground and the tail rose up until my aircraft was upside down. Eventually it came to a stop.

He undid his straps, fell out of the cockpit onto his head and tried to stand up, whereupon one of the British Spitfires roared back, so Inan dived under the tail until the RAF machine left the scene. Abd al-Rahman Inan had crashed not far from the Israeli settlement of Dalia, next to the cleansed Palestinian village of Daliat al-Ruha about 15km west of Ramat David.

British accounts of a third REAF attack are the only ones which exist because both Egyptian Spitfire pilots were killed. These state that at around 0915 two REAF Spitfires appeared. One of them saw a Proctor of the RAF Levant Communications Flight that was preparing to land but now turned towards Haifa, pursued by the Egyptian Spitfire. The RAF standing patrol of two No. 208 Squadron Spitfires flown by Flying Officers McElhaw and Hully went to assist the Proctor but were promptly recalled to Ramat David where they saw another Spitfire. According to McElhaw;

> I saw a single Spit turning over the airfield and came in behind it.... It had clear Egyptian markings and, terrified of precipitating a diplomatic incident, I called the tower telling them that it was an Egyptian and asking if I could shoot it down. The CO said something like 'Yes, get him'. Meanwhile, this chump dives for the deck and nips up a narrow valley in the hills, at about 15 feet [5m].... Well, my excess speed was so great that I had to cut the throttle to avoid overtaking him. I gave him three short bursts from close up and he just went straight in. It was the first time I had ever done any air-to-air firing.

By then the other Egyptian Spitfire, having returned from pursuing the Proctor, had made one attack, dropping a single bomb which fell next to a RAF Dakota which burst into flames. When told that another Spitfire was attacking Ramat David, McElhaw and Hully hurried back to see the second REAF Spitfire, its green and white markings clearly visible, preparing to make a second attack run. McElhaw continued his story;

> He [the Egyptian pilot] just ignores me [probably thinking that the British Spitfire was his colleague]. I break away. Les [Hully] takes a pot at him, then I put in a longish burst. Some bits come off and down he goes. He made a good bang when he hit the ground as he still had one bomb on.

The first REAF Spitfire to be shot down by McElhaw was probably that of *Qa'id Sirb* Sa'ad Sadiq al-Duwayni who reportedly

REAF officers listening with respectful attention to an unnamed Egyptian politician in Cairo during the Palestine War. The *Qa'id Firqah Jawwiyah* (Air Commodore) in the centre is probably Abd al-Muna'im al-Miqaati. (Dr. David Nicolle collection)

The Westland Lysander serial number 516J, of No. 3 Squadron, REAF, loaded with bombs during the Palestine War of 1948. (Dr. David Nicolle collection)

There appears to be no record of Sa'ad Sadiq al-Duwayni being buried at al-Majdal, which might indicate that he was not killed outright and that his body was interred elsewhere, if only temporarily. One obituary stated that 'On 22nd May 1948, he had to raid an enemy site, he took his aeroplane and flew to the assigned target. He flew at a low altitude to be more accurate in his attack, he successfully bombed his target but his plane was attacked and he was injured and he passed away shortly [afterwards].'

Air Vice-Marshal Dawson, the Air Officer Commanding Palestine, was the first senior RAF officer to be informed of the Egyptian attacks on Ramat David. He promptly informed Air Vice-Marshal Dickson, the RAF Air Officer Commanding Mediterranean and Middle East. As it happened the REAF's Chief Operations Officer, *Qa'id Liwa* Salih Mahmud Salih, was in Dickson's office at the time. Both men were appalled and Mahmud Salih said that it was clearly a serious error by the REAF which had been informed that Ramat David was still occupied by the British. He quickly telephoned REAF HQ in Cairo, explained what had happened and was assured that there would be no further attacks. Quite when this call was made is unknown and might have been shortly after the third and final pair of REAF Spitfires took off. Mahmud Salih then rushed back to al-Arish, having been told that the British would prepare a retaliatory force if further Egyptian attacks were made. In fact, the impact on relations between Britain and Egypt was not as bad as might have been expected. Nevertheless, for as long as the Haifa Enclave continued to exist, the British insisted that there must be no further overflying within a 32km radius of Haifa by the REAF.

died slightly later, presumably as a result of his injuries. The pilot of the second REAF Spitfire could hardly have survived such an explosive crash and so was probably *Qa'id Asrab* Muhammad Nasr al-Din Zaghlul. Egyptian records show that all save one of the fallen REAF Spitfire pilots were buried at al-Majdal, their remains presumably handed over to the Egyptian authorities by the British, Israelis or Palestinians. Abd al-Rahman Inan was also announced as missing in action and it was a long time before information reached Egypt that he was a prisoner of war in Israeli hands. This news was eventually passed to *Qa'id Liwa* Ahmad Abd al-Raziq who, like Abd al-Muna'im al-Miqaati, had been one of the Egyptian Air Force's first three pilots and retained close links with the British.

In the meantime the Egyptian government promptly made a formal apology. A letter written by Spitfire pilot Tim McElhaw to aviation historian Brian Cull and passed on to the author stated that;

> The most interesting aspect of this affair is that it received no publicity whatsoever. It was not until 1972 that I found out the truth from Air Chief Marshal Dawson. He said that at that

stage the last thing the government wanted was to embarrass the Egyptians... Apparently the REAF CAS [Abd al-Muna'im Miqaati], who was an old chum, had phoned him, offering to fly up in his white Spitfire to apologise in person. Dawson told him not to bother, as he would never survive the trip [because the British personnel at Ramat David were so angry], and it was left at that.

Miqaati would not have used a Spitfire, white painted or otherwise, but he may have intended to fly to Ramat David in one of the REAF No. 3 (Com.) Squadron's silver doped Lysanders.

In later Egyptian accounts of the tragedy, Salih Mahmud Salih was far more critical of the British, perhaps reflecting the worsening relationship between Egypt and the UK during the intervening years. He wrote that;

Five Spitfires, of the total of eight at al-Arish, flew to follow up the [initial] attack on Ramat David. Once there, they fell into an ambush planned by the British, who launched a surprise attack on the Egyptian aircraft and shot them down. It would have been easy for the British to warn the Egyptian aircraft of their mistake, thus avoiding the damage, but the British, as it appeared, preferred a bloody mass murder, which assisted the Jews in weakening Egyptian air power.

Feelings were similarly bitter on the British side, with the Operations Record Book of No. 6 Squadron stating that; 'The Palestine situation has taken another and very tragic turn, as a result of which the long-suffering British received further casualties at the hands of the irresponsible, undisciplined rabble, apparently completely lacking in any kind of [military] intelligence, known as the Royal Egyptian Air Force.' This collapse in trust also coloured Ali Muhammad Labib's account, published in 1977 when he accused the British of handing Abd al-Rahman Inan over to the Israelis after capturing him. Labib must surely have known this was untrue, as Inan's account of his adventures had been published in Cairo six years previously.

The Egyptian Ministry of Defence issued an official communique which was broadcast from Cairo at 2200 hrs, stating that;

The Royal [Egyptian] Air Force had planned to attack the Zionist airport of Megiddo, six km south-west of al-Afulah. The aircraft left at 0530, but owing to bad weather conditions they missed the Zionist airport and raided the British airport of Ramat David, which lies at the same distance south-west of Nazareth and on the same longitude as the Megiddo airport [in fact slightly further west], causing losses in lives and aircraft. We lost five aircraft.

While the Ramat David incident convinced the Israelis to improve their own airfield defences, its impact upon the surviving members of the REAF Tactical Air Force at al-Arish can well be imagined. Those lost had included some of the most qualified, experienced and respected men in the REAF, Sa'ad Sadiq al-Duwayni apparently having been particularly popular. A somewhat colourful obituary said of him;

War changed him completely, from a normal calm 'eagle' to a boisterous one who obliterated the enemy targets. Nevertheless, his merciful heart never left him even in the most critical situations and he never dropped his bombs on innocents. If he did not find his correct target he would roll and spin, rise and fall, until he identified the military target, which he then destroyed totally. He used to say that enemy ground fire did not bother him at all as it just revealed their position and made it easier to hit them.... If any of his colleagues advised him to rest, he used to shout; 'I am King Faruq's soldier; intense and stressful work is my comfort zone.'

A more questioning account of Sa'ad al-Duwayni's death would be written by his brother and appeared in the magazine *Al-Musawwar* on 3 November 1950 entitled *Those Martyrs – Who is Responsible for their Death?* It is worth quoting at length;

Perhaps the achievements of the Air Force might interest me more than other branches of the military because I had a brother who is now considered one of the martyrs. The authorities are [currently] investigating with officials the losses of life caused by the ammunition.... which exploded in our chests, so is it also the right time for the authorities to investigate those responsible for the loss of the lives of our young men through neglect and disregard of the sacred responsibilities entrusted to them?

Sa'ad al-Duwayni's brother then turned to the Ramat David incident;

This incident would never have happened without the carelessness of the high ranking ---- [the name of the accused officer was deleted in the published article], who had ignored an important message from the British Army warning the Egyptian Air Force against bombing a certain aerodrome because it was [still] a British aerodrome, not an Israeli one.

That high rank [officer] left the message on his desk and did not warn the Egyptian Air Force commanders and as a result, the next morning everything was finished. The Egyptian fighters had bombed the aerodrome that they been warned not to and four pilots were shot down and my brother was one of them.

Are the lives of our pilots so cheap that this made the high rank so lazy in performing his duties, when he could have saved their precious lives?....

Is it possible to call this martyrdom? Is it possible for fighters to lose their lives due to being shot down by a country they are not in war with? No Sir, this is not martyrdom and I do not consider my brother a martyr; I consider him a victim of a trust that was placed in a faulty place.

Following his crash Abd al-Rahman Inan, like Gamal Irfan before him, had tried to make his way to friendly territory, and with a similar lack of success. He returned to his crashed Spitfire and noticed that if it had slid a few more metres, it would have tipped over a cliff into a deep valley. There were also bits of his machine scattered across the hillside. Having retrieved his maps, Inan fired his pistol into the Spitfire's fuel tank but it refused to catch fire. He then refilled his gun but left the first chamber empty so he would have to think twice before shooting.

Inan put the weapon inside his clothes set off towards Jinin, hoping to reach Iraqi lines. It was now 0915 hrs on 22 May and, injured and dazed, Inan remembered little except the rising sun, a stream tricking down the mountainside and the singing of birds. Only after he had walked for some time did the Egyptian pilot notice blood running down both legs of his flying suit. Once he considered that he was far enough away from his crashed Spitfire, Inan decided to spend the night inside one of the piles of harvested wheat which stood around this cultivated zone.

Abd al-Rahman's account of his attempt to reach Arab-held territory, his arrest by remarkably young Israeli militiamen, the latter's quarrelling over the money they found in Inan's pockets, their horror at also finding a Koran deserves to be translated and published. In fact, Inan's caution in leaving the first chamber of his pistol empty saved his life when one of these over-excited youngers pointed the weapon at the pilot's chest and pulled the trigger. First, he was taken back to his crashed Spitfire at which point he heard the bombs of the third and final REAF attack on Ramat David. Eventually the Egyptian was marched across the mountains, was briefly incarcerated behind a metal door, was treated kindly by a Jewish child from Romania whom Inan rewarded with his woollen pullover, and eventually found himself in the Sarona camp on the edge of Tel Aviv.

Compared with the dramatic events involving the REAF, the activities of the RIrAF, the SyAAF and Israeli Air Force were neither very significant nor very exciting. At 0915 hrs GMT one Arab broadcaster announced that; 'The Baghdad Ministry of National Defence, in a communique on military operations of 22nd May, states that the Iraqi Air Force attacked the two settlements of Ashdot Ya'akov and Menahemia, causing great damage and setting them on fire.' At 2000 hrs GMT on the 22nd, Syrian Army Communique No. 8 reported that; 'Our aircraft scored direct hits on Afikim, Kinneret and Jisr al-Sha'iriah [unidentified] and returned safely to their bases.' Meanwhile the Israeli Air Force still held the initiative at night, the Tel Aviv Squadron aircraft bombed 'French Hill' and Kfar Azaria (al-'Isawiya?) on the northern edge of Jerusalem on the night of 22–23 May. On the same night and again on that of 23–24 May, Israeli aeroplanes bombed the village of Iraq Suwaidan and the nearby police fortress, as well as al-Majdal on the coast.

23 MAY 1948

Ground Operations

Despite the catastrophe which befell the REAF the previous day, the Egyptian Army maintained its pressure on various Israeli positions on 23 May, especially Yad Mordechai, with or without air support. Here, at 1745 hrs, the 2nd Battalion mounted its first coordinated infantry-armour assault and after fierce fighting, the Egyptians broke through the Israeli defences to seize part of the settlement.

At noon, on what had become known as the central front, two companies of the Transjordanian Arab Legion launched an attack on Israeli positions in the area of the Mandelbaum Gate following an artillery bombardment. The rest of the 3rd Regiment meanwhile assaulted Israeli positions around Notre Dame Monastery. However, the alerted enemy repelled these attacks, inflicting significant losses upon the 3rd Regiment. Of the 200 infantrymen who had set out to attack Notre Dame at noon, nearly half were either killed or were stretcher cases. So General Glubb, who believed that the seizure of this position did not warrant further casualties, called off any further attack. He was satisfied that, by gaining control of the Old City and most of the remaining territory around the Jewish New City, he had achieved his primary objective.

Elsewhere Lieutenant Colonel Habis al-Majally, commander of the Legion's 4th Regiment, had established firm control over a significant section of the Tel Aviv to Jerusalem road near Latrun, Dayr Ayyub and Bab al-Wad. Further east, units of the 2nd Regiment blocked this same road at Biddu, effectively cutting off the New City. Glubb now decided to wait until the Jews were either starved out of the New City or boundary lines were established by a peace settlement.

Meanwhile, as supplies ran out, it became clear to the Israeli government that the population of New Jerusalem was near the limits of its endurance. This situation convinced *Haganah* high command to undertake a major operation to seize Latrun to break the Arab stranglehold along the strategic road linking Tel Aviv and Jerusalem. The plan called for coordinated attacks by two brigades. The Israeli 7th (armoured) Brigade supported by the second battalion of the Alexandroni Brigade would carry out the main assault from the west while the Harel Brigade launched a secondary attack from the east to secure the eastern section of the Latrun-Jerusalem road. By 23 May, the 7th Brigade was therefore concentrated near Khulda and Na'an, while a large supply convoy at Ekron stood ready to move up to Jerusalem. The actual assault was planned for shortly after midnight on 25 May but due to the late arrival of the Alexandroni battalion, the attack would be delayed.

Air Operations

The suggestion that *Qa'id Sirb* Abd al-Rahman Inan's Spitfire was captured intact is clearly wrong, though parts of it may have been used as spares. The REAF Tactical Air Force had now lost seven or perhaps eight Spitfires, with four pilots killed and three captured. Furthermore, the worst damage had been inflicted by the Egyptians' supposed friends, the British, rather than their Israeli enemies. Indeed, from now on the REAF High Command's main priority was at all costs to avoid another clash with the British,

Muhammad Abu Zaid, kneeling and still with the shoulder insignia of a *Qa'id Sirb*, with four of his REAF colleagues and a civilian who was probably a news reporter, at al-Arish at the start of the Palestine War. (Abu Zaid family archive)

inevitably inhibiting future REAF operations. The ban which the British had imposed on Egyptian machines coming anywhere near Haifa was strictly enforced by the Egyptian government and may have remained in place even after the British evacuated the Haifa Enclave. On the other hand, some Iraqi and perhaps Syrian aircraft did occasionally operate in this area.

In the immediate aftermath of the Ramat David incident there are said to have been only five operational Spitfire 9s at al-Arish under the command of *Qa'id Asrab* Muhammad Abd al-Hamid Abu Zaid, supported by Tahir Zaki who had recovered from being brought down 'between the lines' on 18 May. Nevertheless, the Tactical Air Force still tried to find and destroy the elusive Israeli Avia S-199s while continuing to support Egyptian and Transjordanian ground forces, bombing Israeli concentrations and fortified settlements. Over the next few days Negba would be attacked six times, Dorot and Be'erot Yitzhak four times, Gat twice, Shdemot, Burair, Gvar'am, Kfar Yona, Kfar Haim and the Israeli bases around al-Sarafand and Rishon-le-Zion once each. To support Arab Legion units in Latrun and Dayr Ayyub, Israeli concentrations in the Jerusalem Corridor were similarly attacked six times while, in an effort to maintaining air superiority, Aqir was attacked twice and Sde Dov was attacked once.

Meanwhile additional fighter aeroplanes were rushed to al-Arish, reportedly including some Spitfire Vs, but even before they arrived the Tactical Air Force was probably back in action on 23 May. While it is possible that an official Egyptian communique to this effect at 2200 hrs on the 23rd was referring to earlier sorties for propaganda and morale raising purposes, it referred to one or more raids by REAF Dakota 'bombers' and claimed that;

> The Air Force attacked the fortifications of Taluh [unidentified] with heavy bombs, causing a large explosion and fire. Thick white smoke was observed, constantly increasing. Our planes left their objective on fire. Our planes also successfully raided the fortifications of the settlement of Shdemot, registering direct hits. Our planes attacked a group of enemy lorry concentrations, causing some damage. All our aircraft returned from these operations successfully.

On the other hand, Labib's statement that Egyptian pilots continued operations as soon as new pilots and fighters arrived from Cairo suggests that there was a brief pause or reduction in Spitfire operations.

Once the immediate shock had passed, the REAF selected additional Spitfire pilots to send to al-Arish. The names of several are known and although the list is incomplete, they included al-Abady, Khalil Jamal al-Din al-Arusi, Yahya Husayn, Galal Husayn, Yahya al-Aidarus, Musalhy, Mustafa, Safwat, Mukhtar Mahmud Sa'id, al-Tarazi, Mustafa al-Utaify, Wahdan and al-Wasaimy. Two Lysander pilots mentioned in the Operational Diary had probably been there from the start. They were Ra'uf and Wafa'.

At 1330 hrs on the 23rd, a broadcast from Cairo quoted a communique issued by the Transjordan Government, stating that Egyptian aircraft had bombed a colony near Samakh. However, this target lay immediately south of Lake Tiberias and so the aircraft involved were unlikely to have been from the REAF, more likely being Syrian, unless the BBC Monitoring Service misheard this broadcast. The SyAAF was certainly in action in this area on this day, Syrian Army Communique No. 9 broadcast from Damascus at 2050 hrs announcing that; 'Our planes have successfully raided the settlements of Kinneret and the Kinneret group, as well as Degania. The *Haganah* HQ was hit and a large section of it destroyed.'

Meanwhile the last British Spitfires finally left Palestine, three from No. 32 Squadron and nine from No. 208 Squadron flying from Ramat David aerodrome to Nicosia in Cyprus. Several had been damaged in the REAF raids but all arrived safely. Some ground crews were transported by Dakotas while other personnel travelled overland in a convoy to Haifa, this convoy also towing a more damaged aeroplane, and thence aboard ship. Subsequently the British Admiralty Monthly Intelligence Report for June 1948 recorded that, by 0030 hrs on 23 June;

> Some 70,000 troops with 50,000 tons of equipment, 4,000 police and 5,000 civilians had been satisfactorily embarked, also 9,500 vehicles and 260,000 tons of stores. A further 8,000 vehicles and 60,000 tons of stores had been disposed of locally and 576 armoured vehicles and 4,000 tons of ammunition had been destroyed or sunk at sea.

On the night of 23–24 May one or more Galilee Squadron aircraft crossed the frontier to bomb a Syrian Army HQ at al-Qunaitrah as well as Syrian troops at Kafr Harib and Fiq on the Golan Heights.

24 MAY 1948

Ground Operations

Yad Mordechai eventually fell to the Egyptian Army on 24 May after hard fighting. However, an Egyptian radio communique at 2200 hrs may have been referring to an incident at Yad Mordechai the previous day when it reported an Israeli Air Force attempt to resupply an enemy settlement 'surrounded by our forces,' claiming that this aeroplane was brought down by Egyptian anti-aircraft fire.

Tahir Zaki and colleagues from the REAF Tactical Air Force (including Wing Commander Abu Rabi'a), in the battered Israeli settlement of Yad Mordechai, shortly after it fell to Egyptian assault of 24 May 1948. (Taher Zaki archive)

Tahir Zaki and Abu Rabia in front of the capture kibbutz Dayr Sneid. (Taher Zaki archive)

Syrian soldiers in northern Palestine of 1948. (Albert Grandolini collection)

There is no Israeli record of such a loss but the leader of a *Palmach* commando battalion which arrived in Yad Mordechai during the night of 23–24 May in armoured vehicles, decided that, despite a ferocious 10-hour battle, it was no longer possible to prevent the settlement's collapse. The Israeli garrison therefore evacuated Yad Mordechai at 0315 hrs in the morning, leaving behind 26 dead. Also on 24 May, regular Egyptian troops took over Iraq Suwaidan village and police fort, blocking the main road to Israeli settlements in the Negev. Nevertheless, to say that these Israeli positions were now isolated would be to overstate the case.

During the evening, Israeli forces tried again to save the now-desperate Jewish Quarter within the Old City of Jerusalem, but this attack was again repulsed with 60 *Palmach* troops being killed. Major al-Tal of the Arab Legion had previously been satisfied with bombarding the besieged Jewish Quarter with mortars and artillery fire. Now, as the Jewish defenders still refused to surrender, he decided to take the area by force and to avoid undue losses ordered that enemy fortifications be demolished one at a time.

Under cover of mortar fire and with artillery support from the Mount of Olives, Arab Legion infantry forced the Jewish defenders from position to position and house to house. Because the *Haganah* failed to relieve the Jewish Quarter, white flags started to appear on roofs while two aged rabbis approached the Arab positions carrying a white flag. However, Major al-Tal was not prepared to compromise and insisted that all weapons must be handed over. All able-bodied men would be taken prisoner while women, children and the aged would be sent to the largely Jewish New City. The wounded, depending on the extent of their injuries, would either be held prisoners or be received by the Red Cross. After several days' negotiations, the garrison of the Jewish Quarter finally surrendered on 28 May.

No such terms were offered by Israeli forces to Palestinian civilians when they were overrun, with yet another alleged war crime being carried out by Israeli military or paramilitary forces on 24 May 1948.

Air Operations

The last act of the Ramat David drama came in 24 May when the British handed the aerodrome to the Israelis who paid £5,000 for the existing facilities. The first Israeli Air Force unit to move in was the Galilee Squadron which had been forced from its previous base at Yavn'eel by Syrian Harvards. The British evacuation of the Haifa Enclave did not, however, bring an end to the British desire to know what was happening inside Palestine. Henceforth a series of photo-reconnaissance sorties were flown by Mosquitos of No. 13 Squadron, the first being on 24 May. That same day No. 32 Squadron also flew a reconnaissance mission over Tel Aviv, being fired at over Sde Dov aerodrome and over Aqir.

Whereas the Egyptian communique which claimed REAF raids on 23 May might be treated with some caution, Egyptian Communique No. 13, broadcast at the usual time of 2200 on the 24th was much more straightforward. It stated that;

> Our heavy bombers [usually meaning Dakotas], under a protecting umbrella of our fighters, made several raids, using high explosives. Fuel dumps and oil-stores north-east of Tel Aviv, as well as the harbour and electric power station, received direct hits and fires were started. Bombs were rained down on the barracks south-east of Tel Aviv, which are the main camp for training Zionist forces. Our heavy bombers also attacked the industrial area of Ramat Gan [on the eastern edge of Tel Aviv] and water supplies, causing heavy explosions and leaving the area on fire. All our aircraft returned safely to their bases from all these operations.

Arab aircraft were similarly active in the north, where the Israeli settlement at Kinneret was attacked, the defenders claiming to have

De Havilland Mosquito PR 34 serial number RG190 of No. 13 Squadron RAF in Egypt, reportedly in 1948. (Albert Grandolini collection)

The Yarden Hotel in Tel Aviv after it had been requisitioned for use as the Israeli Defence Force/Air Force headquarters. This building was the target of at least one raid by REAF Spitfires, and perhaps also by Egyptian C-47 Skytrain/Daktoa 'bombers.' (Shlomo Aloni collection)

hit one aircraft which then made a forced landing in Transjordan. It was probably an Iraqi machine, perhaps an Anson, though there is no confirmation from Arab sources.

According to the Voice of Israel radio station broadcasting from Tel Aviv at 1830 on the 24th, Israeli aircraft were active against Syrian targets, claiming that; 'Our planes today bombed enemy concentrations in the Hareb [unidentified] area.' On that day the first sortie by one of the Israeli Air Force's newly arrived Avia S-199 fighters took to the air, either on a test flight or to defend Tel Aviv against REAF bombers. During the following night Gaza and Shu'fat, an Arab suburb of eastern Jerusalem, were also attacked by the Tel Aviv Squadron, causing little if any damage.

25 MAY 1948

Ground Operations

All seemed quiet on the Egyptian front on 25 May, but an Iraqi force struck west from Nablus, past Tulkarm towards Netanya. Somewhat earlier at 0400 hrs, as the first rays of dawn appeared, the Israeli 7th Brigade started its assault west of Jerusalem under cover of 65mm howitzers and a bombardment by 3-inch mortars. The exposed Israeli forces were soon in full view of fully alerted Arab Legionaries in the Latrun area and came under withering fire. Nevertheless, the engagement lasted several hours before the broken Israeli units withdrew, suffering further heavy casualties, the Arab Legion's 4th Regiment troops counting 600 dead in front of their positions. Elsewhere, 25 May witnessed Israeli forces being involved in another reported war crime against Palestinian civilians.

A pair of REAF Spitfires in action low over Tel Aviv in late May 1948. (Dr. David Nicolle collection)

Air Operations

On 25 May the REAF returned to action with a vengeance. It may have been at this point that, to maintain or revive morale, *Qa'id Asrab* Abd al-Hamid Abu Zaid painted the front part of the spinner of a Spitfire V with a piratical black with a white skull-and-crossbones. The list of sorties painted on the front fuselage of another Spitfire 9 is unlikely to have been added at this time, probably being done for a visit to al-Arish by King Faruq and an Egyptian news film-crew during the First UN Truce.

Most REAF activity during the latter part of May still consisted of ground-attack missions in direct support of the Egyptian Army, though targets around Tel Aviv were also attacked. For example, on 25 May, an Egyptian communique, broadcast from Cairo at the usual time of 2200 hrs, stated that REAF 'heavy bombers', supported by fighters, raided the Tel Aviv area and on their way home destroyed several armoured cars near Aqir. The settlements of Be'erot Yitzhak, Givat Brenner and Gat were also bombed along with an Israeli convoy of 14 troop-carrying lorries in Rehovot. All the REAF aeroplanes returned safely.

The night of 25–26 May was nevertheless an exciting one for the men at al-Arish and Gaza, although an Egyptian communique broadcast the following day conflated two separate events, claiming that;

> Yesterday, at 2030, our forces discovered two Zionist aircraft attempting to drop supplies to the Jewish settlement of Bir Haim [unidentified]. Our anti-aircraft guns forced the two planes down and our forces captured them and took the four pilots prisoner. Following this the Zionists launched a night attack in an attempt to recapture the two planes, but our forces beat off this attack....

In fact, a pair of Noorduyn C-64 Norsemen strayed from their flightpath when flying from southern Italy to Israel and headed instead towards Gaza. Their request for guidance was overheard at al-Arish aerodrome where lights were promptly turned on. The C-64 landed whereupon those aboard were arrested. The second Norseman was hit by anti-aircraft fire and came down heavily on a beach near Gaza, its crew also eventually being captured. Although these machines had not attacked any Egyptian targets, Ramallah and an area south of Jerusalem were bombed during one Israeli night sortie while Gaza was targeted by another.

It was around this time that Abd al-Rahman Inan endured his first official interrogation, an Israeli soldier pointing a pistol at the Egyptian pilot and clicking it in a presumed attempt to unnerve the prisoner. Subsequently, Inan was taken to the Hadasaa Hospital in Tel Aviv where his injuries were treated, although some fragments of metal remained in the Egyptian pilot's leg for the rest of his life. He was then taken to Yona Camp where he was put in a small room, three metres square, with a bricked-up window. Mahmud Barakat had already spent some time in the same camp, in a concrete cell where the electric light was never turned off and which had no toilet facilities. One day he heard a voice singing a popular Egyptian song. Barakat took up the tune, the two songsters thereby learning that they were not the only Egyptian prisoner at Yona.

The fact that Abd al-Rahman Inan had survived the Ramat David raids and was a prisoner of war was not made public by the Israeli authorities for some time. On 25 May Inan's obituary was published in the newspapers and a traditional

A Spitfire Mk V of the REAF landing at al-Arish, apparently on an unhardened runway judging by the amount of dust behind the aeroplane. (Dr. David Nicolle collection)

mourning ceremony was held in which the men of the family received those who came to pay their respects. In Abd al-Rahman's case, these included politicians, local government official, senior businessmen and other well-known figures.

Back in the war-zone, the RIrAF was also active on 25 May, an Arabic radio station announcing that;

> The Iraqi Air Force bombed enemy positions in the sector of Kawkab al-Hawa [the ruined Crusader castle of Belvoir], causing considerable damage and silencing its artillery. Planes raided the village of Beit Yusuf [unidentified] for the second time and set it on fire. Enemy concentrations on the road between Gesher and Kawkab al-Hawa were strafed. All our planes returned safely from these operations.

Syrian communique No.11, broadcast from Damascus at 2050 hrs, indicated that the SyAAF was similarly active;

> A squadron of the Air Force attacked enemy lines west of Samakh and dropped bombs on the settlement of al-Manara [probably referring to neighbouring Alumot], setting it on fire. The Air Force also carried out widespread reconnaissance flights in the zone of operations.... A fuel store was also bombed in Degania and set on fire.

Within the newly established State of Israel, there had been shock at the seemingly unopposed Egyptian air raids on Sde Dov aerodrome during the first days of the conflict. An official enquiry was set up which quickly showed that a number of surprising mistakes had been made. This led to further questions and criticisms, but what does not appear to have been mentioned was that the unexpected determination, effectiveness and number of REAF attacks.

At this stage of the conflict, the Israeli Air Force was still mostly active in the hours of darkness, the night of 25–26 May being no different. At 1826 hrs GMT on the 26th, the Voice of Israel radio broadcast that; 'It is reported from Haifa that the Jewish Air Force last night successfully raided enemy concentrations at Sarein [unidentified] and Libba [Libna?] in the north.' A Dragon Rapide of the Tel Aviv Squadron was also to drop supplies to the Jewish Quarter of the Old City in Jerusalem around midnight, but a technical problem delayed its take-off. Eventually arriving over Jerusalem at 0315 hrs, the Dragon Rapide dropped five large packages, only two of which landed in the correct place.

26 MAY 1948

Ground Operations

On 26 May, 11 days after the initial Arab advance into Palestine, the Arab League Political Committee held another meeting in Amman. It was attended by commanders of the various Arab forces in Palestine who were to consider the military situation in the light of another UN Security Council resolution. In fact, the Arab military situation was not as good as it seemed. While most of the missions assigned to Arab forces had been accomplished, the areas they occupied were largely those inhabited by Palestinian Arabs. Meanwhile the main Israeli lines of defence remained intact and several Zionist settlements left behind Arab lines remained militarily active, threatening Arab communications. Furthermore, the forces committed by the Arab governments had proved to be insufficient, lacking in adequate reserves and technical support.

The discussions thus highlighted the need to commit more troops, unify plans and carry out simultaneous attacks from different directions, particularly by Arab Legion, Iraqi and Egyptian troops. The broad lines of the new Arab concept crystallised as follows:

Syrian Army soldiers in a lorry, photographed during the Palestine War in 1948. (Albert Grandolini collection)

(1) The Arab Legion Command had to commit a Brigade Group to besiege Jerusalem and take control of the City. Meanwhile, the rest of its force should move to a concentration area west of Bab al-Wad from where it would be ready to advance against Tel Aviv.
(2) The Iraqi army, after completing its concentration, should move from Nablus to Tulkarm on its way towards Netanya.
(3) The Egyptian army must advance towards Tel Aviv to connect with the Arab Legion force.

As King Abdullah of Transjordan had secretly told the British government that he would refrain from invading areas allotted to the Jewish state, the Arab Legion command informed Major General Nur al-Din Mahmud, the Deputy of the Commander in Chief and representative of the Egyptian Army in Amman, that the Arab Legion was not in a position to launch an attack. They also requested an immediate Iraqi and Egyptian advance to reduce Israeli pressure on Arab Legion units in Bab al-Wad and Latrun. The resulting military confusion would be a major factor in the Arab states' willingness to accept the First UN Truce which came into effect on 11 June 1948.

On the ground, Israeli forces launched another major assault against the Arab Legion force in Latrun on 26 May. To relieve pressure on these Legion units, Iraqi forces were ordered to move against Israeli forces in two directions, advancing towards Tulkarm-Netanya to seize Bayt Lid and the neighbouring crossroad, as well as pushing towards Jinin and Zir'in to capture Lajjun, reaching the former on 27 May. Also on 26 May, Arab Legion units launched a subsidiary operation to secure the Legion's positions west of Jerusalem. At 0345 hrs, a company of the 1st Regiment was sent to occupy Radar Hill, which dominated the Jerusalem road between Abu Ghush and Biddu. Caught by surprise, the Harel defenders were rapidly driven off after which the Legionnaires consolidated their new position.

Air Operations

On 26 May a photograph of a REAF pilot getting into the cockpit of his Spitfire at al-Arish appeared in the most prestigious Egyptian newspaper, *Al-Ahram*. The REAF wanted Egypt and the wider Arab world to know that it was back in business. The REAF also continued to look for the elusive Israeli Avia S-199 fighters and on the 26th the headquarters of the Israeli Defence Forces at Hulda, south of Ramlah, was attacked by Egyptian Spitfires. At nearby Aqir aerodrome Ezer Weizman was told of the attack and leapt aboard one of the Avias, hoping to intercept the Egyptians. He started the engine but a vehicle pulled up in front of his Avia and he was ordered not to take-off. The Israeli Air Force's first fighter squadron was not ready and did not want to give away its position.

The daily communique issued by the Egyptian Defence Ministry broadcast at 2200 hrs GMT on 26 May, confirmed this attack on Hulda where it claimed that two dumps received direct hits, concentrations of soldiers being strafed and heavy losses inflicted. The communique also stated that;

> Our bombers raided the settlement of Shdemot, the bombs reaching their targets. A convoy of lorries and armoured cars, observed near al-Sabta [unidentified] heading for the north, was bombed.... Our aircraft dropped high explosive and incendiary bombs on the Jewish settlement of Be'erot Yitzhak and fires were started in the centre of the settlement. The Jewish settlements of Burair [Bror Hayil next to the 'cleansed' Palestinian village of Burair] and Negba were also raided and big fires were observed, rising to 300 metres. Dense smoke and fire were also observed over the settlement of Negba.... All our aircraft returned safely to their bases....

There appears to have been no mention of combat activity by the RIrAF on Wednesday, but Syrian Communique No. 12, broadcast at 2050 on the 26th, reported that; 'Our Air Force bombed enemy fortifications in Tel al-Kadi [unidentified], destroying it.'

27 MAY 1948

The UN General Assembly had appointed Count Folke Bernadotte as its official Mediator between Israelis and Palestinian Arabs on 20 May. As a member of the Swedish Royal family and a representative of the International Red Cross, Bernadotte had already helped save thousands of Jews as well as Allied prisoners-of-war during the Second World War, especially during the final months.

Now, two days before the UN ceasefire resolution was passed, his white-painted UN Dakota took off from Paris on a long and gruelling tour of Middle Eastern capitals and other cities. The following day the Dakota landed in Cairo and Count Bernadotte began his job as UN Mediator. By the time he had concluded three days of negotiation with King Faruq and the Egyptian government, the UN ceasefire resolution had been passed. Bernadotte then flew to Haifa to hold talks with Israeli leaders. He would also have discussions with General Gordon MacMillan, who was still GOC British Forces in Palestine and Transjordan, and with Air Vice-Marshal Dawson of the RAF. Next came talks with King Abdullah, followed by further discussions with the Egyptian government. After shuttling to and fro in his white Dakota, including a flight to Beirut, Count Folke Bernadotte eventually returned to Cairo on 7 June.

Ground Operations

On the ground, the Egyptian Army's Expeditionary Force in Palestine had been strengthened by the arrival of additional troops in Gaza. This enabled a Second Brigade Group to be formed,

The entrance to the Egyptian Army's Expeditionary Force headquarters at al-Majdal, in Palestine. (Dr. David Nicolle collection)

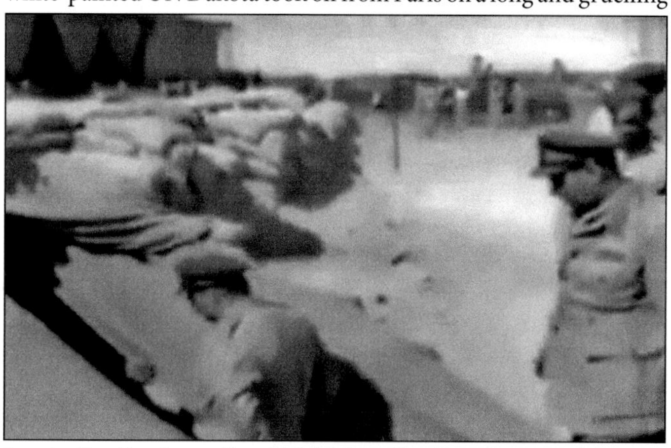

A senior Egyptian Army officer (right) follows King Faruq into one of the underground air-raid shelters constructed at al-Arish aerodrome. (Dr. David Nicolle collection)

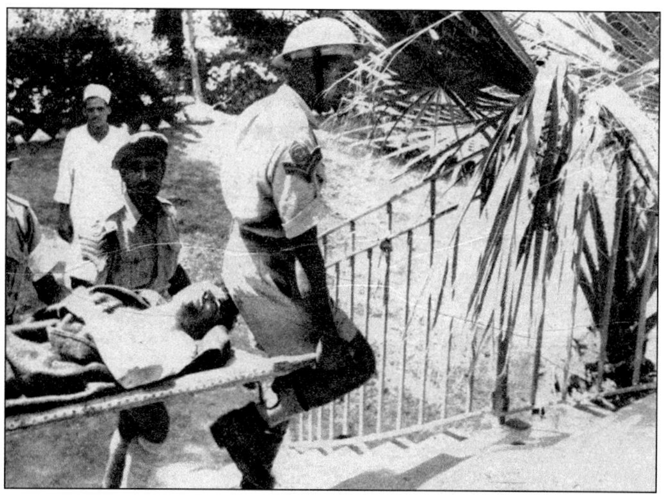

A *Raqib Awwal* (master sergeant) and an *'Arif* (corporal) of the Egyptian Army Royal Medical Corps bringing a wounded soldier into hospital at al-Majdal in Palestine, or more likely in Cairo. (Dr. David Nicolle collection)

consisting of the 1st, 2nd and 9th Infantry Battalions. On 27 May, the Egyptian High Command received an urgent request from Transjordan for immediate Egyptian and Iraqi offensives to reduce Israeli pressure around Latrun. General al-Muwawi was therefore instructed to push northward to seize the line between Isdud and Qastina, a village about 10km to the west. This mission was assigned to the newly formed Second Infantry Brigade Group (2nd and 9th Battalions) while the 1st Battalion strengthened the Egyptian hold on al-Majdal.

Most Egyptian effort was thus focused on the coastal plain between al-Majdal and Isdud, which enabled Israeli forces to take over a deserted British Army camp next to the village of Julis without opposition on the night of 27–28 May. Egyptian forces in neighbouring Julis village would unsuccessfully attempt to retake the camp, and on 11 June Julis village would itself fall to an Israeli assault. Unfortunately, 27 May saw yet another alleged Israeli war crime against Palestinian civilians.

Air Operations

On Thursday 27 May the REAF continued looking for the Israeli fighter squadron, unaware that their quarry was at the ex-RAF aerodrome outside Aqir. However, the usual 2200 hrs GMT Egyptian communique referred to the usual targets, stating that;

> Our aircraft raided the area of Tel Aviv, a Skoda works receiving direct hits, causing a violent explosion.... Our aircraft raided the settlement of Dorot, scoring direct hits on car parks. Our aircraft also attacked the settlements of Be'erot-Yitzhak, Barbara, Negba, Sumsum and Khita [unidentified], inflicting considerable damage. Our aircraft carried out wide reconnaissance operations. All our aircraft returned safely.

Back in Cairo the Egyptian Ministry of Defence and REAF Headquarters were increasingly desperate to get their hands on more combat aeroplanes. Paradoxically this involved selling some that they had already purchased but whose transfer had been blocked by the British embargo. Thus, on 27 May Egypt sold a Spitfire 9 to the Greek government while another was 'struck off charge.' Both these Spitfires, known by their ex-RAF serial numbers PV119 and MH77, were almost certainly held at a British Maintenance Unit, though they were technically now Egyptian property. Both were in an overall aluminium dope finish whereas Spitfires which had been handed over to the REAF were in European theatre grey and green camouflage.

It was also on 27 May that Colonel Frank Ryan, representative of the Association of British Aircraft Manufacturers in Egypt, stated his belief that the REAF would come to a standstill within two months because of its lack of pilots, spares and maintenance facilities. He would be proved wrong, despite the British unwillingness to help the REAF.

There was no mention of Iraqi aircraft in action on Thursday 27 May. But, as on the previous day, Syrian aircraft were, and according to Syrian Communique No. 13; 'Our Air Force bombed a column of enemy cars in the settlement of Kinneret, scoring direct hits. A car carrying ammunition was set on fire.'

Presumably the Israeli decision to move the Galilee Squadron because of persistent raids by SyAAF Harvards had already be made before this latest Syrian attack. The light aircraft of the Galilee Squadron therefore went to the large and far from hidden ex-RAF aerodrome of Ramat David which had protective blast pens and locations for significant anti-aircraft defences. During the following night, 27–28 May, the Israelis used C-47 Dakotas as bombers, their target being Ramallah on the Transjordanian front where they caused little damage.

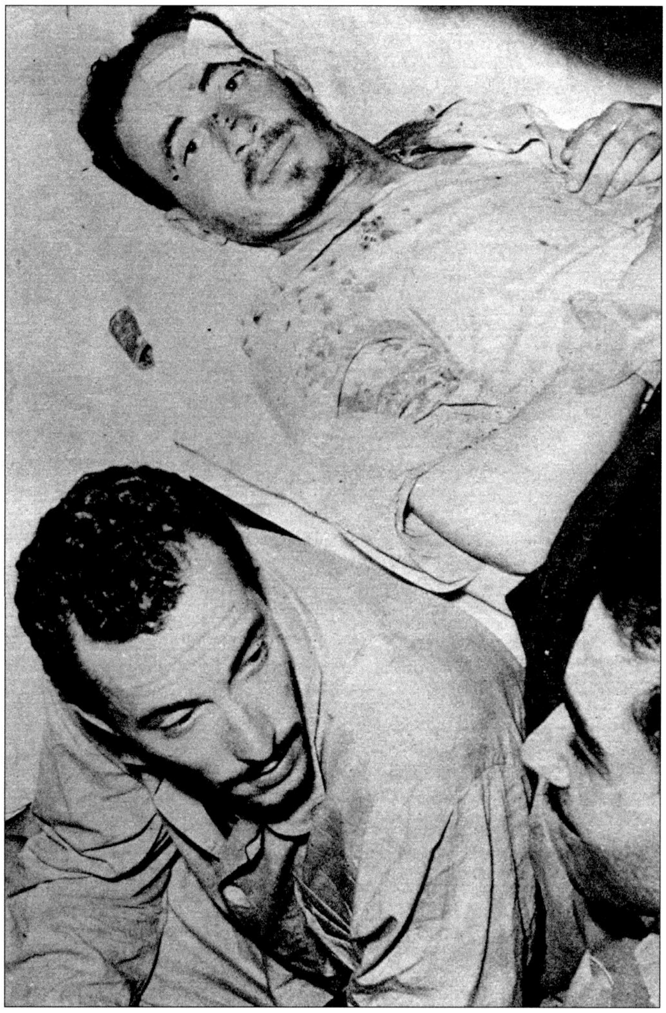

Wounded soldiers, said to include Israelis, in an Egyptian Army field hospital during the Palestine War. (Dr. David Nicolle collection)

28 MAY 1948

Ground Operations

The Egyptian Army appears to have been static on 28 May, busy consolidating its overstretched positions. However, the Iraqi Army struck west from Nablus and captured the Israeli settlement of Geulim. Despite repeated counterattacks on Radar Hill, which was now held by the Arab Legion, the Israelis were not able to recover this key position. Meanwhile, the situation in Jerusalem's New City was so bad that Israeli Prime Minister David Ben-Gurion decided to give priority to the battle to open up what was now known as the Jerusalem Corridor between the Holy City and the Israeli-held coastal plain. On 28 May, Colonel David Daniel Marcus, an American volunteer, was put in command of Israeli forces operating in Jerusalem and this corridor. He would be killed by friendly fire at Abu Ghush on 10 June 1948, his role in the Palestine War later being portrayed by Kirk Douglas in the 1966 Hollywood film *Cast a Giant Shadow* where British 'imperialists' were again portrayed as the main villains with assorted dim-witted Arabs as their stooges.

Also on 28 May, Israeli leaders finally accepted the Arab Legion's terms for the surrender of the Jewish Quarter in the Old City of Jerusalem. Here, at 1400 hrs, they signed an agreement in the presence of Red Cross and UN representatives. For Major al-Tal and his Legionnaires, it was a day of triumph as they received their King's congratulation for saving the Old City and its Holy Sites.

An Egyptian Army armoured car travelling along a road in southern Palestine, showing the lack of cover in this region during the 1948 war. (Dr. David Nicolle collection)

For the Jewish defenders, of course, it was a sad day because they had not only surrendered but had paid such a high cost during the desperate battle. Meanwhile outside the Old City, General Glubb committed another taskforce to clear the Shaikh Jarrah quarter and break through to establish more secure contact with the Old City. The Arab Legion task force given this task was formed of one infantry company and a squadron of armoured cars, supported by four 25-pdr guns, four 6-pdr anti-tank guns and four 3-inch mortars. Elsewhere Israeli forces were yet again accused of a war crime against Arab civilians on the 28th.

Air Operations

During this period the British used the supposedly independent *Sharq al-Adna* radio station to criticise Arab strategy. *Sharq al-Adna* first broadcast in 1942 from Jaffa in then mandated Palestine, but in early May 1948 the station had moved to British-occupied Cyprus. Although *Sharq al-Adna* was regarded by virtually all its listeners as a British mouthpiece, as a creature of the British intelligence services and Foreign Office, its true ownership remained an official secret. Even so, its statements were listened to with interest, not least by Arab military and political leaders, for whom they often contained the official British government view of events.

At 1930 hrs GMT on 28 May, a military commentary in *Sharq al-Adna* stated, somewhat patronisingly, that the activities of the Egyptian Air Force were intensive 'and can prove quite effective in keeping shipping away from the Palestine coast,' thus hindering supplies and arms shipments to the Zionists. In later years *Sharq al-Adna* would become a source of embarrassment to many other British broadcasters. This included the BBC's Arabic Service, where the author (Dr. David Nicolle) worked for several years, and which was desperate to maintain its own reputation for impartiality and independence from the British government.

Meanwhile, Friday 28 May was almost business-as-usual for the REAF at al-Arish, the Egyptians' next official communique broadcast as normal at 2200 hrs GMT;

> Our aircraft, flying over a wide area, reconnoitred large enemy concentrations west of Bab al-Wad, trying to force their way through to Jerusalem to relieve the besieged Zionists. But our bombers launched a continuous attack on these concentrations. High explosives and incendiaries were dropped on the colonies of Hulda and Abu Shusha [probably neighbouring Israeli settlements such as Gezer]. All the bombs were observed to fall on the target, causing fires which could be seen from al-Majdal and Gaza. Thus, the enemy's attempt to relieve the besieged Zionists failed.... Six armoured vehicles near this colony [near Hulda] were strafed, as well as two other cars. All our planes returned safely.

A REAF Spitfire LF.Mk 9 seen on landing, probably at Hilwan or Almaza, rather than at al-Arish. (Dr. David Nicolle collection)

The village of Abu Shusha had first been attacked by the Givati Brigade as part of Operation Barak prior to the declaration of the State of Israel, the first reported massacre of Palestinian villagers being made public by the Arab Legion on 19 May. Two days later an appeal was made to the International Red Cross to prevent 'barbaric acts' which were said to be continuing at Abu Shusha. The last residents who remained in the village following the Israeli conquest were expelled on 21 May. In 1965 the remains of the villages were removed by the Israel Land Administration because they formed what was described as 'a blot on the landscape.'

It later became accepted wisdom that Arab claims in air warfare were exaggerated and that Israeli claims were more reliable. However, this was not the case during the Palestine War. For example, at 1200 hrs GMT on the 28th, the Voice of Israel reported from the central front facing Iraqi and Transjordanian forces that;

> A Rehovot message received today at noon states that Jewish forces in the Latrun area have occupied the two villages of Bayt Jiz and Bayt Susin and have shot down an Iraqi plane which attempted to bomb Jewish positions in that area. Jewish forces also shot down an Iraqi plane in the Jordan Valley.

Both claims seem to lack further corroboration.

A little over 10 hours later a broadcast from Beirut merely announced that 'The Syrian Air Force was very active,' whereas at 2050 Syrian Communique No. 14 broadcast from Damascus had been more specific, stating that; 'Our planes dropped pamphlets from the Arab League on Hula, Tiberias and Acre. Bombs were dropped on the Jewish colony Ashdot Ya'akov and direct hits were scored. Enemy concentrations in Degania Bet were attacked and dispersed.' How accurate these claims were is another matter.

For its part, the Israeli Air Force remained more active after nightfall and during the night of 28–29 May the crew of an Israeli Dakota 'bomber' rolled two tons of relatively small bombs out of the aircraft's cargo door upon the Arab town of Ramallah. Apparently, the Dakota's pilot would bank his aircraft at a suitable moment to make this operation easier. The Israeli Tel Aviv Squadron also attempted to bomb Nablus, Tulkarm and Jinin although the latter target was misidentified and Israeli-held Baysan, was hit instead. Nevertheless, the claim that both sides were now attacking open towns, cities and villages with little effort made to distinguish between military and civilian targets is unfair, certainly in the case of the Arab air forces and probably also of the Israeli Air Force.

29 MAY 1948

By 29 May the UN Security Council was determined to bring the fighting to an end and to establish conditions in which an overall settlement of the Palestine dispute could be considered. Consequently, on the 29th, the Council passed a resolution containing six clear demands:

(1) All governments and authorities concerned had to order a cessation of all acts of armed force for a period of four weeks.
(2) A cessation of hostilities in Palestine would not prejudice the rights, claims and position of either Arabs or Jews.
(3) No government or authority was to introduce fighting personnel or war material into Palestine, Egypt, Iraq, Lebanon, Saudi Arabia, Syria, Transjordan and Yemen during the ceasefire.
(4) The United Nations Mediator for Palestine, in concert with the Truce Commission, had to supervise the observance of the truce.
(5) The State Members of the Arab League and the Jewish and Arab authorities in Palestine had to communicate their acceptance of this resolution to the Security Council not later than 6:00 p.m. (1800 hrs) on 1 June 1948, New York standard time.
(6) Action under Chapter VII of the Charter would be considered if the resolution was rejected or violated by either party or by both.

Ground Operations

The final Egyptian advance northwards started at 0900 hrs on 29 May, with Brigadier General Muhammad Naguib in command of the Second Brigade. Two hours later Naguib's vanguard reached its destination but the main body was moving more cautiously. Nevertheless, the Egyptians met no serious Israeli resistance and reached Isdud during the afternoon. The 2nd Battalion now adopted a defensive posture about 2km north of the town, meaning that they were approximately 35km south of Tel Aviv, while the Egyptian 9th Battalion was deployed in Isdud itself.

On the other side the Egyptian advance had been reported to Colonel Avidan, the Givati Brigade commander, but as Egyptian intentions remained unclear, Avidan tried to consolidate his defensive positions north of Isdud in order to halt any further Egyptian advance. An Israeli forward position was also established near Kfar Warburg, southeast of Isdud, to threaten Egyptian lines of communication. The Egyptian vanguard's push up the coast had reached its furthest point, halting at the destroyed Jisr Isdud (Isdud Bridge) over the Wadi Sukhrir. As a result, patrols from both sides were soon in contact north, east and south-east of Isdud. Some Egyptian patrols probably ventured through the coastal dunes as far as the mouth of the wadi at the tomb of Nabi Yunis and, according to Egyptian Army archives, penetrated to within 25kms of the outskirts of Tel Aviv.

Thereafter, Egyptian military dispositions in Palestine were consolidated, Colonel Naguib being responsible for the day-to-day movement of front-line Egyptian forces. The Egyptian 4th Brigade was now spread along the lateral road from al-Majdal to Hebron, stiffening Muslim Brotherhood units in this region. Facing Naguib's 5,000 men were the 4,800 troops of Israel's Givati Brigade. Naguib had attempted to isolate Negba by occupying Hills 113 and 100 astride the 'middle' road from Burair to Julis, just north of the strategic Iraq Suwaidan crossroads. Julis had also been retaken from Israeli forces. Israeli-held Negba was now very exposed, overlooked by Hill 113 to the west, by the Iraq Suwaidan police fort to the south and to some extend by the village of Bayt Affa to the east. Ibdis to the north and Julis to the north-west, though at a lower altitude, were similarly held by Arab forces. Theoretically the Israeli Negev Brigade, holding a huge area south of this road, was thereby cut off from Israeli forces to the north.

On 29 May, the armoured spearhead of the Iraqi force pushing west in the direction of Netanya, reached Kfar Yona, Ein Vered and within 10km of Netanya before it was halted by the Alexandroni Brigade. Another Iraqi force raided Zir'in from Janin which the Iraqis already controlled. On the Lebanese Front during the night of 28–29 May, the armoured cars and trucks of the main Israeli Yiftach force moved from al-Manara without lights, across Lebanese territory before turning south towards al-Malkiyah. However, while approaching its target from the north, this Israeli force encountered a small Lebanese unit. The latter was forced back but the noise of the engagement alerted Lebanese units in al-Malkiyah. Nevertheless, the latter did not have time to reorganise their defences against this unexpected attack from within their own territory.

After a short battle, al-Malkiyah fell into Israeli hands, obliging the Lebanese to abandon Qadas and retreat behind their own frontier. Following these events, the new Oded (Israeli 9th) Brigade replaced Yiftach troops in the north, while the latter were transferred south to reinforce Israeli forces in the central front. In the meantime, the Lebanese prepared to regain al-Malkiyah, an

Tahir Zaki and an unknown colleague are greeted on their return to al-Arish from a successful mission, probably staged for the benefit of a visiting news cameraman. (Dr. David Nicolle collection)

infantry battalion from the 3rd Regiment supported by six light tanks, four armoured cars and an engineering company were committed to this mission in cooperation with an Arab Liberation Army force.

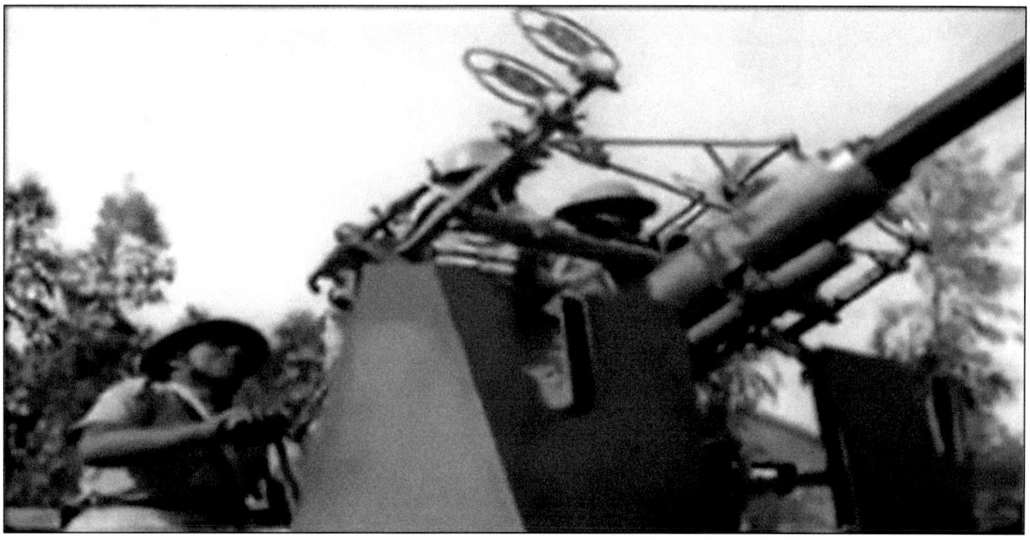

A 40mm Bofors light anti-aircraft gun of the Egyptian Army seen on a 1948 newsreel from Palestine. (Dr. David Nicolle collection)

Air Operations

Egyptian Dakota 'heavy bombers' were again in action on Saturday 29 May against what the official Egyptian communique called the coastal defences of Tel Aviv, claiming 'great damage.' The Israeli General Staff camp at Ramat Gan on the eastern side of Tel Aviv was similarly attacked by REAF Spitfires. On this occasion it is possible that Egyptian Spitfire pilot Tahir Zaki's recollections may again have conflated two attacks, this and another on 8 June when he claimed that the presence of some senior Israeli officers amongst the casualties was confirmed by Israel Radio.

The official Egyptian communiques merely stated that;

> Our Air Force made wide reconnaissance operational over the coastal areas and over the settlements of Be'erot-Yitzhak, Shdemot, Dorot, Gvar'am, Gat, Hamamah [presumably meaning the neighbouring Zionist settlement of Nitzanim], Shoval, Negba and Bureir [meaning the neighbouring Zionist settlement of Bror Hayil]. Our aircraft bombed nine vehicles in the settlement of Be'erot-Yitzhak, all the vehicles being hit, as well as a large depot. Our aircraft dropped incendiary bombs and machine-gunned the settlement of Dorot, damaging three armoured vehicles.

The regular Egyptian communique at 2200 hrs GMT added that; 'The areas of Beer Haim [unidentified] and Gvar'am were raided by our Air Force.... One of the aircraft made a forced landing behind our lines but the pilot returned safely to his base.' According to reports in the Cairo daily newspaper *Al-Ahram* and in the English language *Egyptian Gazette* newspaper, the aeroplane which made a forced landing had been attacking Tel Aviv, which is probably incorrect, and came down inside Egyptian lines.

On this occasion there are detailed corroborating stories from both sides. The diary of Yehuda Rotshield, who lived in Gvar'am, included the following passage;

> On this date a pair of REAF Spitfires attacked Kibbutz Gvar'am around noon. One of the kibbutz's defenders Eliezer Levy opened fire with a local improvised twin-barrel MG-34 gun at the diving aircraft. Missing the leader who dropped a bomb on the kibbutz, he hit the second Spitfire during its dive run. The stricken Spitfire did not manage to climb back from his dive as usual, meanwhile the leader circled above watching the event unfold. The doomed Spitfire was seen flying low, moving as a drunk man, losing altitude until it vanished beyond a nearby hill, 3kms south of the kibbutz [south-east according to another Israeli source]. It crashed in an Egyptian-conquered region.... In the afternoon some Egyptian vehicles were spotted around the crash site. After that, flames were seen rising from the crash site. The people in Gvar'am assumed that since the Egyptians were not able to rescue the aircraft, they chose to burn it so that it would not fall into Israeli hands.

On 14 June 1998 an article entitled *Ants' Nest* appeared in the Egyptian magazine *Al-Tubar* and was by an unnamed, retired Egyptian Army officer. He wrote; 'We were marching from Gaza to al-Majdal. I was riding a jeep and I learned from an Egyptian artillery Humber [armoured car] patrol that an Egyptian fighter plane had been brought down near the area that the pilot Tahir Zaki [previously] came down.' The unnamed officer was taken to the area in an armoured car. 'There we found the pilot Yahya Husayn, slightly injured with his face covered in blood, so I took him to al-Majdal and after a brief rest he returned safely to al-Arish aerodrome.' Yahya Husayn seems not to have flown operationally for a while, next appearing in the Tactical Air Force Diary on 25 June.

On the northern front Syrian Communique No. 15 broadcast at 2050 hrs GMT, stated that; 'Our Air Force bombed the settlements of Harrawi, al-Nabi Yusha', al-Malikiyah, Qadas and Nahariya. Many direct hits were scored causing great fires, especially in Harrawi and Nahariya. An enemy motor convoy was machine-gunned near al-Malikiyah.' This information was essentially the same as that in an earlier Lebanese broadcast which had reported that; 'The Syrian Air Force then made consecutive raids at dawn on enemy positions, particularly armoured cars, which caught fire and remained burning long after the raids.'

More significantly, the Israeli Air Force's newly operational fighters made their first offensive sortie on 29 May, four Avia S-199s from Aqir attacking Egyptian forces as they moved northwards along the coastal road. Little damage was inflicted and one Israeli aircraft was shot down. The claim that this Israeli air attack caused the Egyptians to halt their advance is clearly exaggerated, but there can be no doubt that the appearance of moderately potent Israeli fighters did cause concern to the Egyptian command.

Israeli Air Force staff officers had originally planned to attack the main REAF aerodrome at al-Arish with five aircraft. Egyptian air superiority during daylight hours meant that photo-reconnaissance had not been possible. So Aharon Remez and Ezer Weizman tried to extract information from the three captured REAF pilots, with a notable lack of success.

After the four available Avia S-199s emerged from beneath their camouflage netting, the Israeli pilots took to the air at 1945 hrs, each machine carrying two 70kg bombs. But instead of striking al-

Wreckage of the S.199 piloted by Eddie Cohen, shot down on 29 May 1948. (al-Ahram)

Arish, they were sent against the vanguard of the Egyptian Army column threatening Tel Aviv. The Israeli Avias flew in pairs led by Lou Lenart with Modi Alon as his wingman, followed by Ezer Weizman and Eddie Cohen. Lenart and Alon struck first then headed home. When Alon landed, his undercarriage failing to come down properly, resulting in a ground loop which badly damaged the Avia. Weizman and Cohen struck next, but Eddie Cohen was hit by Egyptian groundfire and crashed about 2.5km from the ex-RAF aerodrome of Qastina (now Hatzor). Two platoons of Israeli troops hurried to the site but the Egyptians got there first.

Subsequently the Egyptian press claimed that the Israeli attacks caused only one fatality with one person injured, accompanying this report with a photograph of Egyptian soldiers holding up part of Cohen's aeroplane. An Egyptian account of the Avia's attack had already been given in an official communique broadcast late on 29 May, stating that; 'Two enemy planes attacked our forces in the area of Isdud in the afternoon. Our anti-aircraft guns shot down one aeroplane in flames and probably damaged the other to the extent that it could not reach its base.' It is in fact possible that Egyptian groundfire damaged the undercarriage mechanism of Modi Alon's Avia S-199, causing it to fail on landing.

The location of the Avia base at Aqir could no longer be hidden and unconfirmed Egyptian sources claim that it was attacked shortly afterwards. Israeli sources maintain that the first Egyptian attack came on 1 June, when REAF Spitfires destroying a hangar and caused several casualties, though the Avia S-199 fighters survived. What is certain is that the Avia squadron soon moved north, to a newly prepared airfield near the orange groves of Herzliyya, either on the last day of May or the first of June.

The Israeli fighters' first combat sortie may not have been particularly successful but it was credited, rightly or wrongly, with a temporary halt in Dakota bombing attacks on Tel Aviv harbour and nearby factories. It was followed by a night raid on the Egyptian Army column by the IAF's Tel Aviv Squadron and before dawn on the 30th by an Israeli C-46 Commando while on its way to Zatec in what was then Czechoslovakia. Elsewhere, Israeli light aircraft supported ground forces engaged with Lebanese troops near al-Malikiyah and Qadas.

30 MAY 1948

Strain between the Syrian military command and the Syrian government had been increasing since Syrian forces joined the effort to save Arab Palestine, largely because of frustration within the Army. At the end of May these came to a head and Prime Minister Jamil Mardam unsuccessfully tried to replace Lieutenant Colonel Husni al-Zaim, the Chief of the Syrian General Staff. Continuing discontent had an obviously detrimental effect upon Syrian morale throughout the rest of the Palestine War while relations between Husni al-Zaim and Jamil Mardam remained tense.

The Israeli army now attempted another assault against the Arab Legion defenders of Latrun, again directed by Colonel Marcus and involving the 7th Brigade supported by a fresh Givati battalion. The initial attack by the 7th Brigade's armoured battalion was followed by an infantry assault while Givati troops supported by one company from the 7th Brigade attempted to seize the village of Dayr Ayyub and its heights east of Latrun. The Israelis then intended to advance to Yalu, thus blockade the Legion's supply route to Latrun. To secure the right flank of the attacking force, two infantry detachments from the 7th Brigade had already occupied the villages of Bayt Jiz and Bayt Susin south of the road, before launching the main assault.

On 30 May, the Israeli forces advanced towards their assigned objectives but when the Givati battalion reached the heights of Dayr Ayyub it came under fire from the front and flanks, many soldiers being killed or wounded. Panic ensued and the Givati battalion withdrew in disarray, leaving behind 137 dead. Meanwhile, the armoured battalion led by Major Haim Laskov was approaching Latrun from the other side. Unaware of the Givati battalion's unauthorised withdrawal, Laskov attempted a combined infantry-armoured assault upon Latrun itself, but withering fire from Arab Legion defenders halted the Israeli infantry companies who failed to follow the armoured unit. Having failed to capture the police station, Laskow was now obliged to withdraw leaving behind four

A Syrian Army soldier with a captured Israeli Sten gun in northern Palestine in 1948. (Albert Grandolini collection)

Soldiers of the Egyptian Expeditionary Force in southern Palestine priming grenades. (Dr. David Nicolle collection)

burned out vehicles and 50 dead. Latrun remained in Arab hands and the supply situation in Israeli-held New Jerusalem remained critical.

Meanwhile, the Iraqi Army seemed the only Arab force to attempt an advance on 30 May. Here units which had taken Jinin also attempted to capture Lajjun but failed. The Iraqis therefore adopted a defensive posture along a front about 10km south-east of al-Afulah. Iraqi armoured cars had nevertheless reportedly attacked Kfar Yonah, just east of Netanya, threatening to reach the coast and thus cut Israel in half.

This day finally saw the completion of the British evacuation of Palestine, with the Union Flag being hauled down in the Haifa Enclave as Supermarine Seafires of the Fleet Air Arm circled overhead. The British AOC and GOC then boarded HMS *Phoebe* and sailed away, to the relief of virtually all involved.

Air Operations

Although the Egyptian Army had come to a standstill, this was certainly not the case with the REAF. At 2200 hrs GMT on 30 May Cairo broadcast Official Communique No. 19, which stated that;

> Today the region of Rehovot was subjected to a heavy raid by the Royal Egyptian Air Force. At dawn our heavy bombers [Dakotas] and fighters [Spitfires] carried out several continuous raids on this area, causing several explosions and leaving most of the district on fire. At midday today, air raids were stopped for two hours, owing to weather conditions. Air activity was resumed subsequently with the same intensity and it was observed that fires were still burning in many places as a result of previous raids. The Royal [Egyptian] Air Force continued its large-scale reconnaissance operations in the south of Tel Aviv. Our planes raided the settlement of Hulda [south of Ramlah] and bombed ten lorries south of this settlement. They also raided the Hulda area, where they destroyed several trucks. Our planes returned safely to their bases from all these operations.

Other sources confirm that REAF activity ranged from Tel Aviv in the north to the area of Ruhamah in the south.

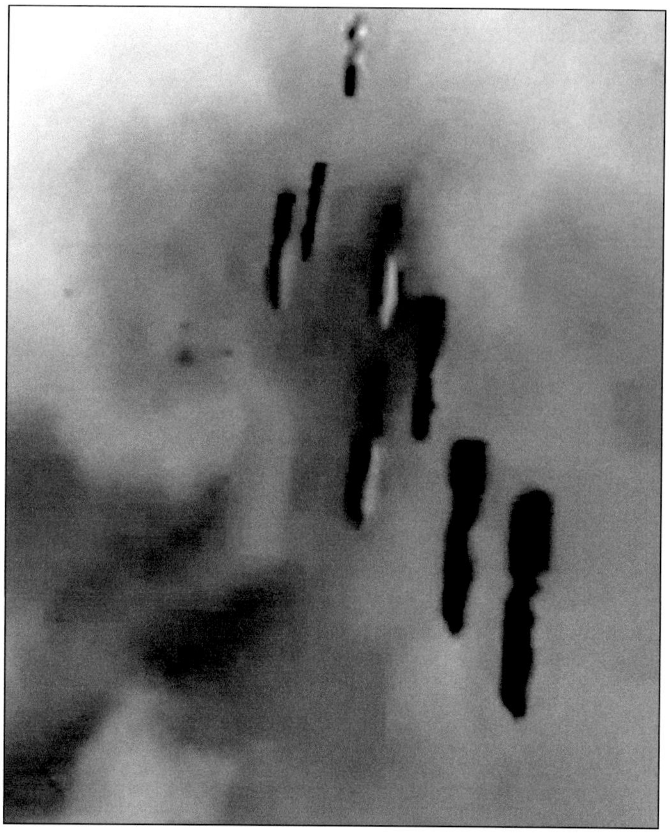

Bombs dropping away from beneath one of the REAF's C-47 'bombers.' Said to have been photographed during a raid on an Israeli target in 1948, it is more likely to have been taken during a training sortie. (Dr. David Nicolle collection)

Officers of the REAF acting as extras, along with two C-47 Dakotas, during the filming of *A Girl from Palestine* at Almaza in the summer of 1948. The presence of Tayyar Thani Mustafa Wagdi Fadil on the far left suggests that these young men included some who were completing their advanced training at this time. (Dr. David Nicolle collection)

The ex-RAF aerodrome of Aqir in south-central Palestine, later renamed Tel Nof by the Israeli Air Force, reportedly seen here during the 1948 war. (Dr. David Nicolle collection)

The other Arab air forces do not appear to have crossed the front lines on this day, but the Israeli Air Force was almost as active as the REAF, its two remaining operational Avia S-199s being sent against the Iraqi push which threatened to cut Israel in half. They took off at 0530 hrs, flown by Ezer Weizman and Milton Rubenfeld, and bombed the railway station at Tulkarm before strafing a nearby Iraqi Army column. Rubenfeld's Avia was damaged by anti-aircraft gunfire, though some Israeli sources suggest he dropped his bombs from such low altitude that their explosions damaged his own machine. He now headed for the coast where he baled-out over the beach north of Netanya, being injured in the process. Weizman's aircraft was also damaged, its windscreen reportedly being shattered by a bird-strike, though he landed safely at Aqir where bullet-holes were found in the Avia's wings.

According to Syrian Communique No. 16, broadcast at 2050 hrs GMT on 30 May; 'An Air Force squadron carried out a heavy raid on the settlement of Nahariya, north of Acre, destroying important positions and sinking a steamer in the harbour. Our planes inflicted heavy losses on the enemy retreating from the village of al-Malikiyah.' It is worth noting that, according to the BBC Monitoring Service, this Syrian communique did not specify that the aircraft involved were Syrian. There are, in fact, several unanswered questions about air activity over this part of the battlefield. An Israel Army Communique, broadcast by the Voice of Israel at 1825, claimed that on what it termed the Sharon Front;

> An Israeli fighter brought down an enemy Spitfire in an air duel over Tulkarm yesterday. Our Air Force attacked enemy concentrations in this sector and hits were scored on guns as well as on four Sherman tanks. This morning also the enemy was attacked by the Israel Air Force in the Tulkarm area.

The following day, at 1045 hrs GMT, the Voice of Israel quoted from an Israeli Army Communique which claimed that; 'Two more Egyptian aircraft were shot down yesterday, one over Gvar'am and one in the Negev.'

The only Arab Spitfires were those of the REAF, and this force did not admit any loss on this day. However, the *Egyptian Gazette* reported that SyAAF aircraft dropped large numbers of leaflets south of Lake Tiberias on 30 May, though there is no evidence that the SyAAF suffered a loss. On the other hand, after being absent from the skies over Palestine for a while, RIrAF Avro Ansons bombed Israeli positions at al-Afulah and neighbouring Merhavia in the Jezreel Valley later in the day. It would seem unlikely that an Israeli fighter pilot would mistake a twin-engine Iraqi Anson for a single-engine Spitfire. No. 7 Squadron RIrAF, whose Ansons were based at Mafraq in northern Transjordan under Lieutenant Colonel Muhammed Ra'uf Hassan, did lose two of its aircraft at the very end of May or during early June, seemingly without fatalities. Both were probably amongst the machines sent to Transjordan to strengthen the RIrAF presence, one crashing in Transjordan as a result of engine failure, while the other crashed at the H3 landing ground in western Iraq.

Other activity by the Israeli Air Force on 30 May was reported by both Transjordanians and Palestinians. A broadcast by the former at 1715 hrs GMT stated that; 'A Jewish aircraft flew over the New Gate area [of Jerusalem] but a strong anti-aircraft barrage compelled it to

A battery of Egyptian field artillery in action during the Palestine War. (Egyptian Ministry of Defence)

A column of universal carriers of the Egyptian Army (popularly known as Bren gun carriers) driving along a road in southern Palestine. (Dr. David Nicolle collection)

A radio operator of the Syrian Arab Army in 1948, tapping out a message using Morse-Code. (Albert Grandolini collection)

retreat,' while a broadcast by the latter at 1300 hrs GMT on 31 May reported that; 'At 1900 yesterday, a Jewish aircraft raided Ramallah, dropping a few bombs and injuring three civilians. At 2215, another Jewish aircraft bombed Lydda, killing two inhabitants and injuring eight.' Other sources mentioned an otherwise unrecorded attack by a solitary Israeli Avia on Egyptian positions at Iraq Suwaidan, causing no apparent damage if it took place at all.

During the following night the Tel Aviv Squadron was again in action, extracts from an Israeli Army Communique broadcast by the Voice of Israel and monitored by the BBC at 1825 hrs GMT the following day stating that; 'Aircraft of the Israeli Air Force attacked military objectives in Ramlah last night. Israel aircraft and artillery also bombed and shelled the enemy at Lydda.... Last night aircraft of the Israel Air Force attacked enemy concentrations at Jinin.' To further confuse the issue, the Voice of Israel earlier reported at 1715 hrs GMT on the 31st that; '*Haganah* made a night attack on large Egyptian Army concentrations near Isdud, our Air Force scored direct hits. One of our aircraft is missing.' The missing aircraft was presumably the Avia of Milton Rubenfeld who had been brought down by Iraqi fire on 30 May, unless the supposed Spitfire brought down by an Israeli fighter was actually a victim of 'friendly fire.' Sadly, the night of 30–31 May 1948 witnessed yet another alleged Israeli war crime against Arab civilians.

This stretch of countryside, photographed from a REAF C-47 Dakota in 1948, appears to be somewhere in the Nile Delta rather than in southern Palestine during a bombing raid as claimed. It was probably taken during a training mission, on the way to the REAF's bombing range. (Dr. David Nicolle collection)

31 MAY 1948

Ground Operations

Egyptian Communique No. 20, broadcast at 2200 hrs GMT, considered the most worthy news to be the capture of a pilot who had apparently been on the run for several days. However, even this poses unanswered questions, especially where the identity of man is concerned. According to this broadcast; 'One of our patrols succeeded in capturing the fifth pilot, who escaped into the woods, from the two Zionist aircraft forced down by our artillery on 25th May. The pilot is William Maxim, an American Christian.'

Douglas C-47 Dakotas of the REAF at al-Arish aerodrome during the Palestine War. (Dr. David Nicolle collection)

Air Operations

In contrast to the lack of dramatic activity on the ground, the REAF remained very busy. Again according to Egyptian Communique No. 20;

> Our heavy bombers [C-47 Dakotas and perhaps also C-46 Commandos] and dive bombers [a new description of REAF Spitfires] continued to pound the area of Rehovot.... A large quantity of high explosives and incendiary bombs was dropped, reaching the targets and causing fires. Our heavy and light bombers [the latter perhaps referring to ground-attack Spitfires], escorted by fighters, raided the airfield of Aqir and bombed the hangers and grounded aircraft, scoring direct hits. Fires broke out. The settlement of Gat was also raided; high explosive and incendiary bombs were dropped and petrol storage tanks were set ablaze. Two aircraft raided the settlements of Be'er Tuvia and Qastina, bombing important targets and setting them on fire. All our aircraft returned safely to their bases.

A Douglas C-47 Dakota of the REAF landing at al-Arish in 1948. It might be one of the machines painted an overall light brown to be used as both bombers and transports. (Dr. David Nicolle collection)

On the other side, the IAF's only remaining operational Avia S-199 was back in action when Modi Alon escorted Tel Aviv Squadron Dragon Rapides on a daylight bombing mission against Arab Legion positions near Latrun, the site of the Israeli army's recent defeat. From their prison camp, Abd al-Rahman Inan and his captured comrades could see Israeli fighters taking off from their new home at Herzliya. Presumably referring to an earlier or a later date, he recalled that; 'We used to observe Messerschmitt planes take-off and land in this airport no more than two kilometres away [actually further than this], we follow them till they disappear behind a row of trees, flying at low altitude rocking their wings joyfully.'

Some of Inan's other memories were more painful and concerned conversations with prisoners who had witnessed or survived brutal massacres by Israeli troops, militias or other paramilitary forces. He was particularly upset by the Red Cross's inability to carry out proper investigations and how they were misled by the Israeli officials who accompanied them.

In contrast, Inan and his REAF colleagues were treated

In the film *A Girl from Palestine*, the hero is the commander of an Egyptian Spitfire squadron who, having been injured in combat, takes over the leadership of a heavy bomber unit. In this sequence he is helped from his Spitfire V by real REAF personnel acting as extras. (Dr. David Nicolle collection)

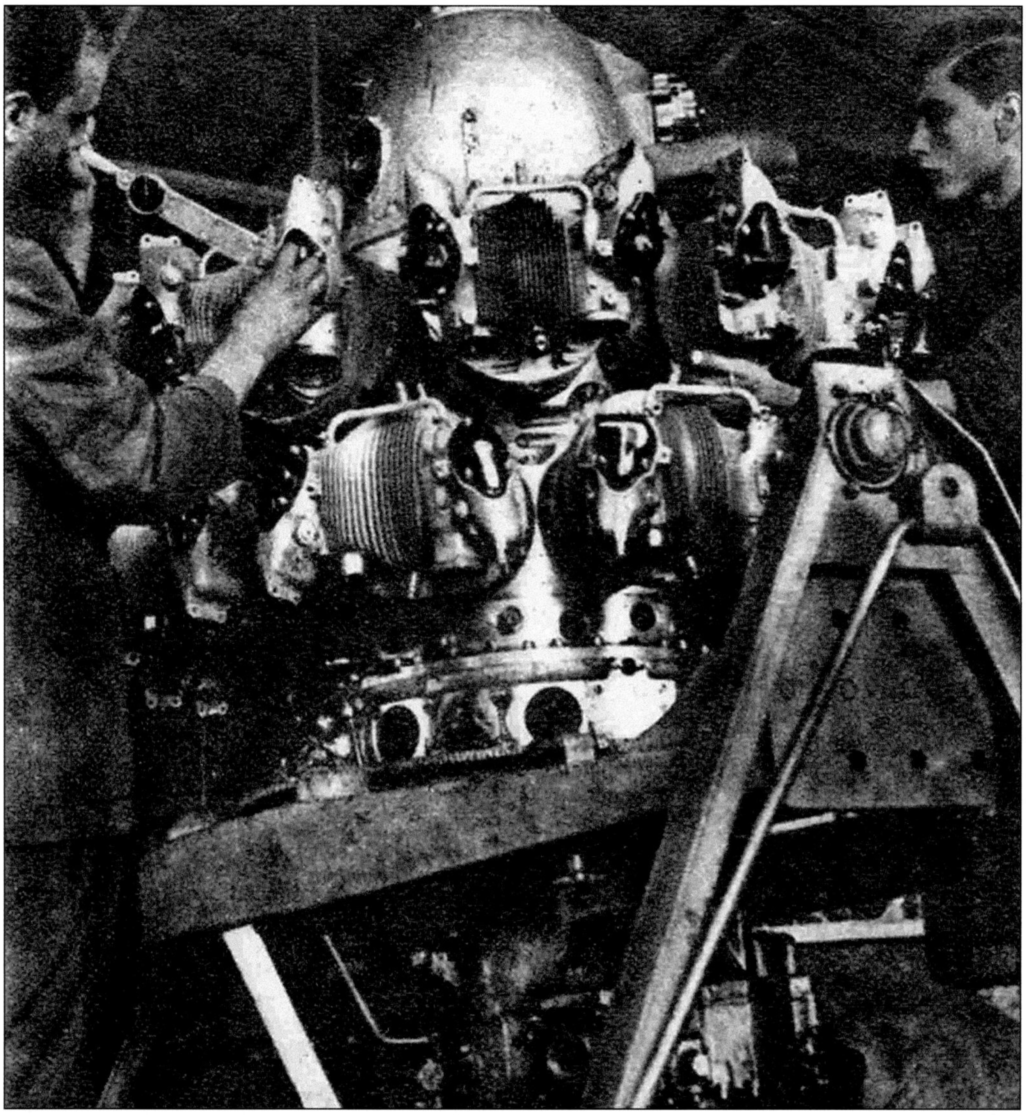

An engine, reportedly from one of the REAF's C-47s, being overhauled by Egyptian engineers. The photograph was published in the REAF 'In House' magazine on 8 September 1948. (Dr. David Nicolle collection)

moderately well. The location of their prison camp nevertheless put them in danger. An attack on Herzliyya airfield by their REAF colleagues, perhaps on 31 May or 1 June damaged two non-operational Avias. It was probably during this raid that the prison guards abandoned their charges. As Inan recalled;

> One morning we were going to shower when a bomb fell close to us. The [Israeli] soldiers looked at each other in fear and anxiety then, when a second bomb fell even closer, the soldiers ran rapidly away. Those who were shaving stopped shaving and those who were showering cleared soap from their eyes and ran to a non-target [?]. He who was in the toilet put on whatever he had as fast as possible, then fled without knowing where his feet led him. As for us [prisoners], we watched what was happening with mockery and contempt. It was not a raid on the [POW] camp, but was aimed on the neighbouring aerodrome. How this raid warmed our hearts!

The REAF raid had achieved complete surprise and according to Inan, the ground defences did not fire a single shot;

> Shimtoff [one of the Israeli guards] commented that 'These fighters have mistaken their target', the shrapnel scattering within the walls of the camp, knowing that there was no military site near it. At that moment, two fighters of Messerschmitt type approached and landed one after the other in a close formation. We watched them until they disappeared behind a grove of trees, then turning to Shimtoff to answer him, but he had gone.

At 2050 hrs GMT a radio broadcast from Damascus quoted Syrian Communique No. 17, announcing that;

> A squadron of our Air Force raided the Jewish settlement of [next to] al-Afula. Direct hits were scored, causing heavy losses. Another squadron of our Air Force attacked enemy concentrations between Kafr Kama and Yavn'eel. Car parks west of Yavn'eel were machine-gunned and most of the cars were set on fire.

This confirmed an earlier statement on *Voice of Israel* which reported that; 'The village of Zir'in, which we had conquered, was bombed from the air; there were no casualties. The settlement of Kinneret was bombed by the enemy.'

In this tense atmosphere, the British RAF found itself called upon for what No. 6 Squadron's Operations Record Book described as an incident of interest; namely providing an escort 'for a special Dakota, chartered by the United Nations Organisation to fly the leader of the International Red Cross, Count Bernadotte, to Haifa from Cairo.... A section of four aircraft, led by F/L B.J. Sprace, D.F.C., met the Dakota over Ismailia, and escorted it safely to Haifa without incident.'

Thus ended the first two weeks of the Palestine War of 1948–1949: unknown to almost everybody involved, much more fighting – and yet more tragedies – were to follow over the next six months. That story is to be continued in Volume 11 of *Air Power and the Arab World*.

BIBLIOGRAPHY

BOOKS

Abu-Sitah, Salman H., *Atlas of Palestine 1948* (London: Palestine Land Society, 2004)

Ali, F.K., *Al-harb al-'Arabia al-Israilia 1948-1949* [*The Arab Israeli War 1948- 1949*] (Beirut, 1982) (in Arabic)

Anon., *Tarikh al-Quwat al-Iraqiyat al-Musalat. Al-Jazz' al-Saba 'Ashar. Ta'sus al-Quwwat al-Jawiyah wa Tatwirha* [*History of the Iraqi Armed Forces, Part 10. Establishment and Development of the Air Force*] (Baghdad, 1988) (in Arabic)

Baghdadi, Abd al-Latif al-, *Mudhakirat* [*Recollections*] (Cairo, 1977) (in Arabic)

Be'eri, E., *Army Officers in Arab Politics and Society* (New York: Praeger, 1970)

Cooper, T., & M. Sipos, *Wings of Iraq: Iraqi Air Force, 1931–2003, Volume 1* (Warwick: Helion & Co, 2020)

De Gayffier-Bonneville, A-C., *L'echec de la monarchie egyptienne, 1942-1952* (Cairo: Institut français d'archéologie orientale, 2010)

Goldschmidt, A., A.J. Johnson & B.A. Salmoni, *Re-Envisioning Egypt 1919-1952* (Cairo: American Univ. in Cairo Press, 2000)

Halim, N. Abbas, *Diaries of an Egyptian Princess* (Cairo: Zeitouna, 2009)

Hamlin, J.F., *The de Havilland Dragon Dragon/Rapide Family* (Tunbridge Wells: Air-Britain, 2003)

Ilan, A., *The Origins of the Arab-Israeli Arms Race. Arms, Embargo, Military Power and Decision in the 1948 Palestine War* (New York: New York University Press, 1996)

Imam, Abdullah, *Wagih Abaza, Sahafat min al-Nidal al-Watani* [*Wagih Abaza, Pages from the Nationalist Struggle*] (Cairo, 1995) (in Arabic)

Inan, Abd al-Rahman, *Kanat Isiran*[*I was a Prisoner*] (Cairo, 1971) (in Arabic)

Jabr, Jabr 'Ali [Gabr, Gabr Ali], *Al-Quwwat al-Jawiyah bayn al-Siyasat al-Misriyah wa'l-Isra'iliyah, al-Jazz' al-'Awal 1922-1952* [*The Air Force between Egyptian and Israeli Policies, volume 1, 1922–1952*] (Cairo, 1993) (in Arabic)

Kafafi, M., *Fi Dikhran 15 Mayu 1948. 'Andama Istushihdan Abi! 'Azaf 'alay 'Uwtar al-Dhikra* [*In Memory 15 May 1948. When my Father was Martyred! A Tune upon the Strings of Memory*] (Cairo, 1975) (in Arabic)

Labib, Ali Muhammad, *Al-Quwat al-Thalāthah* (*The Third Force*) (Cairo 1977) (in Arabic)

Lee, D., *Wings in the Sun: A History of the Royal Air Force in the Mediterranean 1945-1986* (HMSO: London, 1989)

Marr, D.S.B., *A History of 208 Squadron* (Southend, 1966)

Marszalkiewicz, J., *Air Combat During Arab-Israeli Wars* (Lublin: Kagero Publishing, 2017)

McGregor, A., *A Military History of Modern Egypt, From the Ottoman Conquest to the Ramadan War* (Westport: Praeger Security International, 2006)

Nomis, L., with B. Cull, *The Desert Hawks. An American Volunteer Pilot's Story of Israel's War of Independence, 1948* (London: Grub Street, 1998)

Nordeen, L., & D. Nicolle, *Phoenix over the Nile. A History of Egyptian Air Power 1932-1994* (Washington: Smithsonian Institution Press, 1996)

Raafat, S.W., *Privileged for Three Centuries. The House of Chamsi Pasha* (Cairo, 2011)

Sayigh, Y., *Arab Military Industry, capability, performance and impact* (London: Brassey's, 1992)

Shakib, I., *Harb filistine, 1948, Ru'iya misriyya* [*The Palestine War, 1948: An Egyptian Perspective*] (Cairo, 1986) (in Arabic)

Sipos, M., & T. Cooper, *Wings of Iraq, volume 1: The Iraqi Air Force, 1931–1970* (Warwick: Helion & Co., 2020)

Smisek, M., *Czechoslovak Arms Exports, Volume 1: Origins, Israel and Jordan 1948–1989* (Warwick: Helion & Co., 2021)

Stuart-Paul, R., *The Royal Saudi Air Force. A Legacy of His Majesty King Abdul Aziz Ibn Saud* (London: BAE Systems in association with Stacey International, 2001)

Sturtivant, R., *The Anson File* (Tonbridge, Air Britain Historians Ltd, 1988)

Vatikiotis, J., *Nasser and his Generation* (London, Routledge, 1978)

ARTICLES AND ANTHOLOGY CHAPTERS

Andersson, L., "Wings Over the Desert: Aviation on the Arabian Peninsula. Part One Saudi Arabia", *Air Enthusiast, 112* (July-August 2004) pp. 39–43

Anon., "How did you join the Air Force?" [recollections of Air General Mahmud Sidqi], *Al-Quwat al-Musalah* (November 1959) pp. 22–23

Anon., "Success story in the sky" [REAF bomber operations in the 1948 War & the experiences of Captain Yussuf Fahmi] (cutting of published article, date unknown; translation supplied by Group 73 Aviation Historians, Cairo)

Badr, Capt. Salah, "Diary of Capt. Salah Badr" [commander of Egyptian Army garrison, Iraq Suwaydan, 1948] translated into Hebrew, *Bamahane* (8 November 1960) pp. 11–13

Baghdadi, Abd al-Latif al-, "Ma qabl al-dubbat al-ahrar [Before the Free Officers]", (in Arabic) *Hadhihi al-Thawra* (Cairo 1953) pp. 188–189

Biyali, Muhammad al-, "At the REAF Operational HQ", *Akher Sa'a* (8 September 1948) (translation supplied by Group 73 Aviation Historians, Cairo, page numbers unknown)

Biyali, Muhammad al-, "Okra Sandwich" [account of a bombing raid on Tel Aviv by REAF Dakotas] (in Arabic), *Akher Sa'a* (8 September 1948) (translation supplied by Group 73 Aviation Historians, Cairo, page numbers unknown)

Deraz, Issam, "Mudhakirat 'an 'Ida' al-l-wa'l-tayar: Tahir Zaki Hassan Zaki [Recollections of Taher Zaki Hassan Zaki]" (in Arabic)' *Al-Manar al-Jadid* (date unknown) (copy of the author's pre-publication typescript provided by Tahir Zaki, 2005)

Mahbub, Ali Muhammad (Lt.), "Conditions of Flexibility in the Tactical Air Force", (in Arabic), *Mujallat al-Silah al-Jawi al-Malki [RAF (Egyptian) Air Force Magazine],* 10 (1948) pp. 17–23

Siddiq, Muhammad Kamil (Major), "Air War in Palestine" (in Arabic), *Mujallat al-Silaj al-Jawi al-Malki* [*RAF (Egyptian) Air Force Magazine*], 10 (1948) pp. 29–31

Taha, Sayyid, Brigadier, (diary extracts from 1948, published in 1950) (in Arabic) (photographed but unattributed cutting supplied by Brigadier Dr. Abd al-Rahman Zaki, 1971)

Zaki, Tahir, "The pilot who attended his own funeral", (in Arabic) *Al-Tubar* (21 June 1998) (cutting supplied by Group 73 Aviation Historians, Cairo; page numbers unknown)

INTERVIEWS AND PRIVATE CORRESPONDENCE

Abu Zeid, S.S., interviewed by the author concerning his uncle, Muhammad Abd al-Hamid Abu Zaid (Alexandria, 2000)

Cooper, T., correspondence concerning the Royal Iraqi Air Force from the 1930s to the 1950s (1997 to 2015)
Gazerine, Group Captain I.H., correspondence & follow-up information on the REAF following an interview with the author (Cairo, 1973–1974)
Hinnawi, Air Vice-Marshal M.S. al-, interviewed by the author (Cairo, 1999)
Kafafi, M., interviewed by the author concerning her father, Adli Kafafi (Cairo, 1999)
Miqaati, Air Commadore M. Abd al-Muna'im al-, interviewed by the author (Cairo, 1973)
Razzaq, Brigadier General A. Abd al-, interviewed by Tom Cooper (supplied to the author, 2007)
Sabri, F., interviewed by the author concerning members of his family in the REAF & EAF (Cairo, 2011)
Shafei, I. el-, interviewed by the author concerning his father Adli al-Shafa'i (Cairo, 2011)
Sidqi, Air Marshal Mahmud [Muhammad Sidqi Mahmud al-Milaigy], anonymous interview in the late 1950s (text supplied by Nour Bardai)
Sulayman, Abd al-Hamid [Suleiman, Abdul Hamid], interviewed in Cairo by Gabr Ali Gabr (Cairo, 1988)
Tawfiq, M. [Mona Tewfiq], interviewed by the author concerning her father Hassan Tawfiq (London 1997 & 1999)
Zaki, Kamal, interviewed by the author (Cairo, 1999)
Zaki, Tahir, interviewed by the author (Cairo 1997 & 1999)

NATIONAL ARCHIVES (LONDON)

AIR 2/4810 – Loan of RAF personnel & equipment to the RIraqAF, 1940–1950
DEFE 4/16/145 – Report on the RIqAF, 11 October 1948
DEFE 5/8/115 – Report on the RIqAF, 7 October 1948
FO 371/69188 – Confidential report on current strength of REAF from British Air Attaché in Cairo, 19 October 1948
FO 371/69223 – Foreign Office on Ramat David and other incidents involving British military personnel from British Embassy in Cairo, 14 June 1948; letter concerning British Ambassador's meeting with the Egyptian Prime Minister, 14 June 1948

ONLINE SOURCES

Aboul-Enein, T., "The Writings of Abdullah Imam on Flight Commander Mohammed Wagih Abaza", *Small Wars Journal,* 845 (26 August 2011): https://smallwarsjournal.com
Andersson, L., *Wings Over the Desert, Aviation on the Arabian Peninsula, Part 2*: http://www.artiklar.z-bok.se/Arabia-1.html
Morris, B., *Arab-Israeli War* [on war crimes during the Arab-Israeli wars]: www.crimesofwar.org/a-z-guide/arab-israel-war

UNPUBLISHED SOURCES

Anon., *Biographical Note on the late Squadron Commander Mohamed Abdul Hamid Abu Zeid* (EAF Historical Department, n.d., supplied to the author 2001)
Anon., *Bab al-Sadis*, Chapters 29–30: "Tactical Air Force operations, pp. 421–437; "Officers who Fell", (in Arabic) p. 504 (Egyptian Ministry of Defence restricted circulation study of operations during the Palestine War, n.d.)
Anon., *Outline of the Career of Qa'id Liwa Jawi (Military Staff) Muhammad Hassan al-Maghribi* (in Arabic) (Egyptian Ministry of Defence, unpublished typescript, n.d.)
Anon., *Struggle and Championship, The late pilot engineer Abdel Hamid Mahmoud (Abd al-Hamid Mahmud) (in Arabic)* (Egyptian Ministry of Defence, unpublished typescript, n.d.)
Anon., *The Faluja Battle* (Egyptian Ministry of Defence, unpublished typescript, n.d.)
BBC Monitoring Service, *Transcripts of Middle Eastern Broadcasts during the Palestine War 1948–49* (BBC Monitoring Service, Caversham)
Fadil, Mustafa Wagdi, *Pilot's log books 1948–49* (selected pages supplied to the author)
Gabr, Gabr Ali, Air Brigadier Dr., *The Arab Israeli Conflict: The Roots and the Wars 1897-1979: An Egyptian Perspective* (unpublished book text, 2007)
Hartoch, N., *A History of the Syrian Air force 1947-1967* (PhD thesis, London University, 2015)
Hinnawi, Shalabi al-, "Eagles of the Air in Palestine" [on the 1948-49 Palestine War] (in Arabic) (unpublished book chapter)
Nadif [Nassif], Faisal, *Diary*, recovered from his body on 16 July 1948 (English translation of Hebrew translation of original Arabic text; supplied by the IDF, 29 November 1995)
Stafrace, C., *The Iraqi Air Force* (pre-publication draft supplied by the author, 2008)
Various., *Operational Diary of the REAF Tactical Air Force [1948-49]* (incomplete photocopy)

ABOUT THE AUTHORS

Dr. David Nicolle is a British historian specialising in the military history of the Middle Ages, with special interest in the Middle East and Arab countries. After working for BBC Arabic Service, he obtained his MA at SOAS, University of London, followed by a PhD at the University of Edinburgh. He then lectured in art history at Yarmouk University in Irbid, Jordan. Dr. Nicolle has published over 100 books about warfare ranging from Roman times to the twentieth century, mostly as sole author. He also co-authored the Arab MiGs series of books which covered the history of the Arab air forces at war with Israel from 1955 to 1973. Furthermore, he has appeared in several TV documentaries and has published numerous articles in the specialised press.

The late **Air Vice-Marshal Gabr Ali Gabr, PhD (EAF, ret.)** served as a pilot of De Havilland Vampire fighter jets during the Suez War of 1956. After concluding higher military education at the Air Warfare Institute in 1960, he served as Instructor in Air Tactics at the Air Warfare Institute in 1962–1964 and 1966–1967, as Staff Officer during the June 1967 War, Chief of Operational Training Branch in 1968–1973 and as Chief of Operations Group during the October 1973 War with Israel. After serving as Instructor in Art of Operations and as Chief of Air Force Chair at High War College from 1977 until 1982 and receiving his PhD at Nasser High Academy in 1989, he moved into writing and published seven books and dozens of studies and articles on history of air warfare in Egypt and abroad.